STUDIES ON THE HOLOCAUST

Selected Writings, Vol. 1

by

Randolph L. Braham

The Rosenthal Institute for Holocaust Studies
Graduate Center/City University of New York
and Social Science Monographs, Boulder

Distributed by
Columbia University Press
2000

EAST EUROPEAN MONOGRAPHS, NO. DXLIX

ISBN 0-88033-447-9
Library of Congress Catalog Card Number 99-76428

Printed in the United States of America

Contents

Introduction

My interest in politics and international relations began in the mid-1930s, at age fourteen, following the outbreak of the Spanish Civil War and the subsequent indirect involvement of Nazi Germany and the Soviet Union. That war was clearly the beginning of the military conflict between the two totalitarian systems that dominated the political scene during much of the twentieth century. I remember having been fascinated by the evolution of that conflict, which after a brief interlude based on the so-called Hitler-Stalin non-aggression pact, came to a climax on June 22, 1941, when the Axis Powers, which had been at war with the Western democracies since early September 1939, attacked the Soviet Union. Like virtually all other Jews and freedom-loving people everywhere, I rooted for the ultimate victory of the Grand Alliance that was established shortly thereafter.

As a victim and survivor of both totalitarian systems—I was in a forced labor service unit with the Hungarian Army for over fifteen months, and, after liberation by the Red Army, in a Soviet POW camp—I became interested in finding answers to some agonizing questions that came to preoccupy my entire professional life—questions relating to the Nazis' war against the Jews and the theory and practice of Soviet communism. In the course of time, the former became a matter of conscience and historical responsibility, while the latter became a major topic in the comparative political science courses I taught and The City College and the Graduate School of the City University of New York.

In connection with the Nazis' attempt to "solve" the Jewish question, I dedicated myself to finding rational answers to many seemingly unanswerable questions: how was it possible to murder millions of people on an assembly line basis during the broad daylight of the twentieth century? What were the many complex factors that made the planning and implementation of the Final Solution originate in Germany, a country that was in the forefront of cultural development and whose Jewish population, proportionately small, was both highly patriotic and assimilated? As a survivor of the Holocaust in

Hungary, in which my parents and many relatives were among the close to 600,000 victims, I naturally became even more interested in finding answers to what, I eventually concluded, was a unique chapter in the Nazis' war against the Jews.

While the Jewish communities of German-dominated Europe were being systematically destroyed, the Jews of Hungary, though subjected to harsh legal and economic measures and a series of violent actions, survived the first four and half years of the war relatively intact. By late fall 1943, when the government of Miklós Kállay was searching for an honorable way out of the war, the Hungarian Jews, almost oblivious to the suffering of the Jews elsewhere, had become convinced that what happened in Poland could not possibly occur in chivalrous Hungary. Neither they nor the conservative-aristocratic elements on whom the Jews had depended for protection envisioned the possibility that Hungary, a member of the Axis Alliance and one of the first supporters of the Third Reich, would become the victim of a German occupation.

Ironically, it was the Kállay government's ill-conceived and poorly prepared attempt at emulating Italy's example and extricating itself from the Axis Alliance that sealed the fate of Hungarian Jewry. The attempt was doomed to failure: the aristocratic-conservative government was maneuvering in secret for a possible separate peace with the Western Allies that would not only assure the avoidance of a Soviet occupation, but also safeguard the independence and territorial integrity of the country, and possibly preserve the antiquated socio-economic structure of the gentry-dominated society.

Aware of these "secret" negotiations, the Germans finalized their military contingency plans early in 1944. The occupation of Hungary on March 19, 1944, was designed primarily to defend the military and economic interests of the Reich. In addition to assuring Hungary's continued loyalty to the Axis, the occupation enabled the SS and their Hungarian hirelings to implement the Final Solution at lightning speed. Time was clearly of the essence, for the Soviet front was fast approaching the borders of Hungary. As a consequence, the Hungarian Jews were subjected to the most ruthless and concentrated destruction process of the war. Within less than four months all of Hungary (with the notable exception of Budapest) was made *Judenrein*. With fewer than 200 men at its disposal, the SS Special

Commando which entered Hungary together with the Wehrmacht, was able to achieve this "victory" in the war against the Jews only with the wholehearted and often enthusiastic collaboration of the Hungarian police, gendarmerie, and civil service.

In contrast to the destruction of the other Jewish communities of German-dominated Europe, the liquidation of Hungarian Jewry took place on the eve of Allied victory, when the secrets of Auschwitz were already widely known and even the Nazis realized that the Axis would lose the war. It was perhaps precisely because of this that the SS and their Hungarian accomplices decided to bring at least the war against the Jews to a "victorious" end.

The studies included in this collection attempt to provide some answers to the questions posed above. The first essay offers a comprehensive overview of the unique features of the Holocaust in Hungary, differentiating it from that suffered by the other Jewish communities in Europe. The second provides a documented account about the time and manner in which the national and Jewish leaders of Hungary became aware of the Final Solution. Unlike the Jewish Council leaders of most other countries in Nazi-dominated Europe, who were generally unaware of the scale and scope of the Final Solution, the national and Jewish leaders of Hungary were fully familiar with the realities of Auschwitz by the time of the German occupation.

The third deals with the Hungarian press of the 1938-45 era, which, with a few notable exceptions, became a potent instrument in the hands of the Right radicals. An integral part of the vehemently anti-Semitic propaganda machine, the press fostered a climate of opinion that conditioned the Hungarian public to acquiesce in the increasingly severe anti-Jewish measures of the successive counterrevolutionary governments, including those enacted during the Holocaust.

A handful of political and military leaders of the radical Right became interested in "solving" the Jewish question in Hungary as early as 1942. As documented in the fourth essay, these leaders were impressed with the Nazis' achievements in Slovakia and elsewhere, and pursued their goal in collusion with the SS in charge of the Final Solution without attracting the notice of the conservative-aristocratic government.

The fifth essay deals with perhaps the most controversial issue of the Holocaust in Hungary: the attitude and actions of the Central Jewish Council of Budapest, whose members were generally familiar with the Nazis' Final Solution way before Hungary's occupation by the Germans. The essay explores the functional characteristics of these leaders both before and during the Holocaust.

The next essay is a historiographical-critical analysis of the memoiristic, scholarly, and periodical literature dealing with the rescue of Jews during the Holocaust in Hungary. The last essay provides a succinct yet comprehensive overview of the postwar war crimes trials that were held in connection with the destruction of Hungarian Jewry. While focusing on those held in Hungary, the essay also deals with the civil and criminal trials that took place in many other parts of the world, including Austria, Canada, Czechoslovakia, Germany, Israel, Yugoslavia and the United States.

There is no other chapter in the history of mankind that is as well-documented as the Holocaust. The literature on the catastrophe that befell Hungarian Jewry was greatly enriched after the collapse of the Communist system in 1989. This was largely due not only to the greater accessibility of the national and county archives, but also to the renewed interest in the subject matter, which was largely taboo during the Communist era. The many monographs and periodical studies that appeared in Hungary complemented those that were published elsewhere, providing new data and insights into many aspects of the Holocaust. While assembling this collection, I was gratified to conclude that none of the essays required fundamental changes. In a few cases I felt necessary to update the text by explanatory notes.

I would like to express my thanks to the editors and publishers for their permission to reproduce the studies included in this volume. I would also like to express my gratitude to my friends and colleagues who have supported my scholarly endeavors during the past decades, especially Gisella and Arie Edrich, Valerie and Frank Furth, Eva and Norman Gati, Irene and Paul Greenwald, Sheba and Jacob Gruber, Ann and Gaby Newmark, Elizabeth and Jack Rosenthal, and Marcel Sand. For their support and encouragement, I would like to express my appreciation to Dr. Frances Degen Horowitz, President of the Graduate School and University Center of the City University of New

York, and to Professor Egon Mayer, Director of the Center for Jewish Studies. I am particularly indebted to my friend Gábor Várszegi, the mentor of the "J. and O. Winter Fund," for his generosity and understanding of the importance of Holocaust studies. For their editorial and professional contribution to this work, I am indebted to Leslie Bialler of Columbia University Press, and especially to my wife Elizabeth.

Randolph L. Braham
New York, NY
July 1999

1

The Holocaust in Hungary: A Retrospective Analysis

Historical Antecedents

The Holocaust in Hungary was in many respects distinct from the tragedies that befell the other Jewish communities in Nazi-dominated Europe. This distinction is reflected in the disastrous set of historical circumstances which combined to doom Hungarian Jewry in 1944.

The destruction of Hungarian Jewry that year constitutes one of the most perplexing chapters in the history of the Holocaust. It is a tragedy that ought not to have happened, for by then—on the eve of Allied victory—the leaders of the world, including the national and Jewish leaders of Hungary, were already privy to the secrets of Auschwitz. Moreover, except for a few diehards who still believed in Hitler's last-minute wonder weapons, even the perpetrators realized that the Axis had lost the war.

The last major phase in the Nazis' war against the Jews, the Holocaust in Hungary is replete with paradoxes. The roots of one of the most startling of these paradoxes can be found in the "Golden Era" of Hungarian Jewry (1867-1918). It was during this period that a cordial, almost symbiotic relationship developed between the aristocratic-conservative and the Jewish elites of Hungary. It was this *very* close relationship, however, that distorted the Jewish leaders' perception of domestic and world politics during the pre-Holocaust era. While the Jewish elites shared the aristocratic-conservative leaders' abhorrence of Nazism and Bolshevism, they failed to recognize that the fundamental interests of the Hungarians were not

---

A version of this essay was first published under the title "The Uniqueness of the Holocaust in Hungary" in *The Holocaust in Hungary: Fifty Years Later*, Randolph L. Braham and Bela Vago, eds. (New York: Columbia University Press, 1985), pp. 177-90.

always identical with those of Jewry. Their myopic views proved counterproductive during the interwar period and disastrous after the German occupation of March 19, 1944.

After its emancipation in 1867, the Jewish community of Hungary enjoyed an unparalleled level of multilateral development, taking full advantage of the opportunities offered by the so-called "liberal" regime that ruled the country during the pre-World War I era. The Hungarian ruling classes—the gentry and the conservative-aristocratic leaders—adopted a tolerant position toward the Jews. They were motivated not only by economic considerations, but also by the desire to perpetuate their dominant political role in a multinational empire in which the Hungarians constituted a minority. Because of Hungary's feudal tradition, the ruling classes encouraged the Jews to engage in business and industry, so that in the course of time a friendly, cooperative, and mutually advantageous relationship developed between the conservative-aristocratic leaders and the Jewish industrialists, bankers, and financiers—a relationship that was to play a fatal role during the Holocaust. The Jews also took full advantage of their new educational opportunities and within a short time came to play an influential, if not dominant, role in the professions, literature, and the arts.

As a consequence of the Hungarian policy of tolerance, the Jews of Hungary considered themselves an integral part of the Hungarian nation. They eagerly embraced the process of magyarization, opting not only to change their names but also to serve as economic modernizers and cultural magyarizers in the areas inhabited by other nationalities in the polyglot Hungarian Kingdom. The Hungarian Jews, who had no territorial ambitions and naturally supported the group that offered them the greatest protection—as did the Jews of the Diaspora practically everywhere during their long and arduous history—were soon looked upon as agents for the preservation of the status quo by the oppressed nationalities clamoring for self-determination and independence.

The Jews were naturally cognizant of the protection the regime provided against the threat of anti-Semitism. The prompt and forceful intervention of the government in dealing with anti-Jewish manifestations, however sporadic and local they were at the time, further enhanced the fidelity of the Jews to the Magyar state.

In the course of time the Jews, especially the acculturated and assimilated ones, became ever more assertively pro-Magyar. In many cases this allegiance was not only because of expediency or gratitude for the opportunities and the safety afforded by the aristocratic-gentry regime, but also because of fervent patriotism. As Oscar Jászi, a noted sociologist and social-democratic statesman, correctly observed, "there is no doubt that a large mass of these assimilated elements adopted their new ideology quite spontaneously and enthusiastically out of a sincere love of the new fatherland." Jászi concluded, however, that the "intolerant Magyar nationalism and chauvinism of the Jews had done a great deal to poison relations between the Hungarians and the other nationalities of the prewar era."[1] Paul Ignotus, a noted publicist, echoed these sentiments, arguing that the Jews had become "more fervently Magyar than the Magyars themselves." A similar conclusion was reached by the noted British historian Robert Seton-Watson, whose sympathies clearly lay with the oppressed nationalities. He claimed in 1908 that "the Catholic Church and the Jews form today the two chief bulwarks of Magyar chauvinism."

It was to some extent the political and economic symbiosis between the conservative-aristocratic and Jewish leaderships during the so-called Golden Era that determined their views and attitudes toward both the Third Reich and the USSR during the interwar and wartime periods. While the Hungarian leaders looked upon the Third Reich as a vehicle for the possible satisfaction of their revisionist ambitions, they shared with the Jewish leaders a fear of both German and Russian expansionism and above all a mortal fear of Bolshevism. It was these attitudes and perceptions that guided both leadership groups during the fateful year of 1944 with almost equally disastrous results.

The signs that the commonality of interests (*Interessengemeinschaft*) between the two groups was in fact limited, fragile, and based primarily on expediency were clearly visible even before the end of World War I: despite the eagerness with which the Hungarian Jews embraced the Magyar cause and the enthusiasm with which they acculturated themselves, they failed, with relatively few exceptions, to fully integrate themselves into Hungarian society. Their ultimate assimilationist expectations were frustrated, for they were accepted socially neither by the aristocratic gentry, which exploited them politically and economically for the perpetuation of their feudal privileges, nor by the disenfranchised and impoverished peasantry, which—like a large proportion of the industrial workers—often viewed them as instruments of an oppressive regime.

Christian-Jewish relations were further strained by the presence in the country of a considerable number of mostly impoverished Yiddish-speaking Jews who resisted assimilation, let alone acculturation. In contrast to the assimilated magyarized Jews, these were pejoratively referred to as "Eastern" or "Galician," and almost by definition unworthy of the government's policy of toleration. During the interwar period these Jews became the target of special abuse, for even the "civilized" anti-Semites regarded them as constituting not only a distinct "biological race" but also an "ideological race" representing a grave threat to Christian Magyars. This perception was shared by Miklós Horthy, the Regent of Hungary, who probably also considered this "threat" when he consented, during his March 1944 meeting with Hitler, to the "delivery of a few hundred thousand workers" to Germany.[2]

The Interwar Period

The *Interessengemeinschaft* between the Hungarian ruling classes and the Jews came to end with the collapse of the Habsburg Empire and the dismemberment of the Hungarian Kingdom in 1918. The short-lived Communist dictatorship that followed soon thereafter had a crucial effect upon the evolution of Hungarian domestic and foreign policy during the interwar period. The brief but harsh period of the proletarian dictatorship headed by Béla Kun left a bitter legacy in the nation at large, and had a particularly devastating effect upon the Jews of Hungary. Although the overwhelming majority of Jewry had opposed the proletarian dictatorship and perhaps suffered proportionately more that the rest of the population—they were persecuted both as members of the middle class and as followers of an organized religion—popular opinion tended to attach blame for the abortive dictatorship to the Jews as a whole. In part, this was due to the high visibility of Communists of Jewish origin in the Kun government and administration; however, it was primarily the consequence of the anti-Semitic propaganda and anti-Jewish activities of the counterrevolutionary clericalist-nationalist forces that came to power later in 1919—forces dedicated to the reestablishment of the status quo ante.

Driven by the so-called "Szeged Idea" (a nebulous amalgam of political-propagandistic views whose central themes included the struggle against Bolshevism, the fostering of anti-Semitism, chauvinistic nationalism, and revisionism—an idea that antedated both Italian Fascism and German Nazism), the counterrevolutionaries engulfed the country in a wave of terror which dwarfed in ferocity and magnitude the Red Terror that had preceded and allegedly warranted it. While their murder squads killed a large number of leftists, including industrial workers and landless peasants as well as opposition intellectuals, their fury was directed primarily against the Jews; their violence claimed thousands of victims.

Radicalized by the national humiliation, social upheavals, and catastrophic consequences of the lost war—Hungary lost two thirds of its historic territory, one-third of its Magyar people, and three fifths of its total population—the counterrevolutionaries organized themselves in a variety of ultrapatriotic associations devoted primarily to the successful resolution of the two major issues that came to obsess Hungary during the interwar period: revisionism and the Jewish question. In the course of time these two issues became interlocked and formed the foundation of not only Hungary's domestic policies but also its relations with the Third Reich.

Following the absorption of historic Hungary's major national minorities into the Successor States, the Jews suddenly emerged as the country's most vulnerable minority group. With the transformation of Trianon Hungary into a basically homogeneous state, the Jews lost their importance as statistical recruits to the cause of Magyardom. In the new truncated state they came to be exploited for another purpose: as in Nazi Germany a little later, they were conveniently used as scapegoats for most of the country's misfortunes, including its socio-economic dislocations.

In this climate it was no surprise that Hungary—the country in which the Jews had enjoyed a "Golden Era" just a few years earlier—emerged as the first country in post-World War I Europe to adopt, in the wake of the White Terror, an anti-Jewish legislation. The so-called *Numerus Clausus* Act (1920), which was adopted in violation of the Minorities Protection Treaty, restricted admission of Jews into institutions of higher learning to six percent of the total enrollment—the alleged percentage of Jews in the total population. Although this particular legislation was allowed to expire a few years later, it sanctified the fundamental principle that was to guide many of the civilized anti-Semites of the 1930s who were eager to solve the Jewish question in an orderly and legal manner. This principle would be formulated by Gyula Gömbös, one of the foremost representatives of the Hungarian radical Right, who stipulated that "the Jews must not be allowed to succeed in any field beyond the level of their ratio in the population."[3]

At any rate, at that time the Jewish leadership viewed the anti-Jewish measures of the counterrevolutionaries merely as temporary aberrations caused by the unfortunate outcome of the war, and retained its patriotic stance. The leadership not only embraced the cause of revisionism, but actually protested and rejected all "foreign" interventions on its behalf—including those by the international Jewish organizations—as violations of Hungarian sovereign rights. And indeed, their optimism was for a while reinforced during the 1920s, when Count István Bethlen, a representative of the conservative-aristocratic group of large landholders and financial magnates that had ruled Hungary before World War I, headed the Hungarian government.

The appointment of Gömbös as Prime Minister in October 1932, coinciding with the spectacular electoral victories of the Nazi Party in Germany, brought the Jewish question to the fore once again. It soon became a national obsession that frequently rivaled revisionism in intensity. Borrowing a page from the Nazis' propaganda book, the Hungarian radicals depicted the Jews as naturally unpatriotic, parasitically sapping the energy of the nation, and prone to internationalist—i.e., Bolshevik—tendencies. The propaganda campaign was soon coupled with demands for a definitive solution of the Jewish question. The suggestions offered by the radical Right at the time ranged from legal restrictions on the Jews' professional and economic activities to their orderly "resettlement" out of the country.

Although expediency and temporary tactical considerations induced Gömbös to "revise" his position on the Jewish question, his policies prepared the ground for the disaster that was later to strike Hungary and its Jews. He tied Hungary's destiny almost irrevocably to that of Nazi Germany. He not only abandoned Bethlen's reliance on the Western democracies and the League of Nations as a means to correct "the injustices of Trianon," but also brought Hungary's foreign policy into line with that of Nazi Germany and made possible the subsequent penetration and direct involvement of the Reich in practically every aspect of the country's life. This was greatly facilitated by the formidable and potentially collaborationist power base Gömbös established during his tenure. He was able not only to replace the civil and military bureaucracies of the state apparatus with his own protégés, but also—and this was perhaps more crucial—to pack the upper army hierarchy, including the General Staff, with younger, highly nationalistic Germanophile officers. The stage for anti-Jewish excesses to come was further set through the radicalization of the press and the flourishing of ultra-rightist political movements and parties.

The spectacular domestic and foreign policy successes of the Third Reich, including the *Anschluss* with Austria by which Germany extended its borders to those of Hungary, were achieved largely because of the shortsighted appeasement policies of the Western democracies. The Nazi victories induced successive Hungarian governments to embrace the Axis ever more tightly. They became increasingly eager to see Hungary involved in the establishment of the "New Order" in Europe and reaping the benefits of the Nazi revisionist-révanchist policies as an active member of the Axis Alliance. The pro-Reich policy was especially supported by the Germanophile General Staff, the Right wing of the dominant Government Life Party, and the industrial-banking establishment, including Jews and converts.

While this policy yielded considerable dividends, enabling Hungary to fulfill parts of its revisionist ambitions at the expense of Czechoslovakia, Romania, and Yugoslavia, it was in the long run disastrous for the country. It was, of course, even more catastrophic for the country's Jews. In retrospect, the policies of the aristocratic-gentry-dominated conservative governments appear to have been quite unrealistic, if not quixotic. Having embraced the Third Reich for its opposition to Bolshevism and its chief bulwark, the Soviet Union, and for its support of revisionism, these governments were soon compelled to come to grips with the ever more influential Right radicals at home. While they despised and feared these radicals almost as much as the Jews—the Hungarian Nazis had advocated not only the need to solve the Jewish question, but also the necessity to bring about a social revolution that would put an end to the inherited privileges of the conservative-aristocratic elements—the governmental leaders felt compelled to appease them as well as the Germans. In fact, these leaders looked upon the Right radicals' preoccupation with the Jewish question as a blessing in disguise, for it helped deter attention from the grave social-agrarian problems confronting the nation. They were, consequently, ready to adopt a series of anti-Jewish measures. These became more draconic with each territorial acquisition between 1938 and 1941. In addition to passing three major anti-Jewish laws—the third one incorporated some of the basic provisions of the Nuremberg Laws of Nazi Germany—they adopted a discriminatory system of forced labor service for Jews of military age, a unique institution in Nazi-dominated Europe.

These anti-Jewish measures of the various governments, endorsed by the leaders of the Christian churches, were based on the illusions that guided the ruling elites until the German occupation. They thought that by passing laws that would curtail the Jews' economic power and "harmful" cultural influence, they could not only appease the ultra-rightists who thrived on the social and economic unrest that plagued the country, but also satisfy the Third Reich and at the same time safeguard the vital interests of the Jews themselves. This rationalization was part of the larger quixotic assumption that Hungary could satisfy its revisionist ambitions by embracing the Third Reich without having to jeopardize its own freedom of action.

The upper strata of Hungarian Jewry, including the official national leadership, shared these illusions, convinced that the Jewish community's long history of loyal service to Magyardom would continue to be recognized and their fundamental interests safeguarded by the ruling elite of the country. They accepted, however reluctantly, many of the anti-Jewish measures as reflecting "the spirit of the times" and as necessary tactical moves to "take the sting out of the anti-Semitic drive" of the ultra-rightists at home and abroad. They tended to concur with the rationalizations of the governmental leaders that the anti-Jewish laws were "the best guarantee against anti-Semitism and intolerance."[4] In consequence, they were convinced that the safety and well-being of the Jews were firmly linked to the preservation of the basically reactionary conservative-aristocratic regime. And, indeed, as long as this aristocratic elite remained in power, the vital interests of Hungarian Jewry were preserved relatively intact.

The Wartime Period

This remained so even after Hungary entered the war against the Soviet Union in June 1941. The Hungarian regime continued not only to provide haven to the many thousands of Polish, Slovak and other refugees, but also consistently to oppose the ever greater pressure by the Germans to bring about the Final Solution of the Jewish question. While the Jews in Nazi-controlled Europe were being systematically annihilated, Hungary continued to protect its 825,000 Jews (including approximately 100,000 converts identified as Jews under Hungary's racial law of 1941) until it virtually lost its independence in March 1944.

The pre-occupation record of Hungary was, of course, not spotless. About 60,000 Jews lost their lives even before the German invasion: over 42,000 labor servicemen died or were killed in the Ukraine and Serbia, close to 18,000 were killed in the drive against "alien" Jews, and about 1,000 were slaughtered in the Bácska area. Nevertheless, Hungarian Jewry continued to dwell in comparative personal and physical safety. There were no restrictions on their freedom of movement and they were treated relatively fairly in the allocation of food. Although the anti-Jewish laws had a particularly severe economic impact on the lower strata of the Jewish population, including both skilled salaried workers and the unskilled laborers, the economic situation of the Jews as a whole was relatively tolerable, primarily because of the well-developed communal self-help system. Also, those in business and industry, while having their activities severely curtailed, were usually able to circumvent some provisions of the anti-Jewish laws or take advantage of loopholes. The relatively few industrial magnates, mostly converts, actually benefited from Hungary's armament program and dealings with the Third Reich.[5]

The situation of Hungarian Jewry appeared to improve in 1943 despite the Nazis' relentless war against the Jews in the rest of German-occupied Europe. Following the destruction of the Second Hungarian Army near Voronezh and the subsequent defeat of the Germans around Stalingrad early in 1943, the Hungarians began a desperate search for an honorable way out of the war, a search that was intensified after Italy's extrication from the Axis Alliance later that summer. It ultimately led to disaster, primarily because of the irreconcilably conflicting political and socioeconomic objectives the conservative-aristocratic leaders were pursuing.

The Hungarian leaders were eager not only to safeguard the independence and territorial integrity of the country, including the retention of the areas acquired between 1938 and 1941, but also to preserve the antiquated socioeconomic structure of the gentry-dominated society. While they were apprehensive about a possible German occupation, they were above all paralyzed by the fear of the Soviet Union and Communism. They viewed the latter as the ultimate evil to which even Nazism, if it proved unavoidable, was preferable. Ignoring the geopolitical realities of the area, they consequently unrealistically tried to solve their dilemma by maneuvering "in secret" for a possible separate peace with the Western Powers. Unaware of the realities of the Grand Alliance, they fervently hoped that the Western Allies would invade Europe from the Balkans and thereby achieve a double military and political objective: the destruction of the Nazi forces and the prevention of Bolshevik penetration into the heart of Europe.

With spies planted in all segments of the Hungarian government, the Germans were fully informed about the nature and scope of the "secret" negotiations between the emissaries of Prime Minister Miklós Kállay and the representatives of the Western Allies in Italy and Turkey. Reports to the Nazis by their many agents in Hungary about the "treacherous and pro-Jewish" activities of the Kállay government were reinforced by two secret memoranda by Edmund Veesenmayer, the German expert on East Central Europe who later became Hitler's plenipotentiary in Hungary.

Veesenmayer warned the Führer not only about the untrustworthiness of the government, but also about the "danger" represented by the Jews. He contended that the Jews were "Enemy No. 1" and that "the 1.1 million Jews amount to as many saboteurs ... who must be viewed as Bolshevik vanguards."[6] In addition, there were weighty military considerations: extrication of Hungary from the Axis when the Soviet forces were already crossing the Dniester would have deprived Germany of the Romanian oil fields and exposed the German forces in the central and southern parts of Europe to encirclement and possibly an immediate and crushing defeat. It was primarily to safeguard their military security interests that the Germans decided to occupy Hungary and prevent it from emulating Italy.

The German Occupation Era

The destruction of Hungarian Jewry, the last surviving large bloc of European Jewry, was to a large extent the concomitant of this German military decision. Ironically, it appears in retrospect that had Hungary continued to remain a militarily passive but vocally loyal ally of the Third Reich instead of provocatively engaging in essentially fruitless, perhaps even merely alibi-establishing diplomatic maneuvers, the Jews of Hungary might have survived the war relatively unscathed. But the fundamental interests of the Hungarians were in conflict with those of the Jews. While the aristocratic-conservative leaders despised the Nazis, they were grateful for the support of the Third Reich in achieving a great part of their revisionist ambitions and mortally fearful of a Bolshevik takeover. Although most of the Jews shared the Hungarians' abhorrence of both Nazism and Bolshevism, they looked upon the Soviet Union—a member of the Grand Alliance—as the only realistic savior from the threat represented by the Nazis and their local allies.

The German forces who invaded Hungary on March 19, 1944, were accompanied by a small but highly efficient special commando unit (*Sonderkommando*) headed by Adolf Eichmann, which had prepared a number of contingency plans to take advantage of any opportunities to "solve" the Jewish question that might be provided by the new Hungarian leaders. Two years earlier, Eichmann had been indirectly approached by some high-ranking Hungarian ultra-rightists to help "resettle" thousands of "alien" Jews, but had refused to mobilize his deportation apparatus for this small-scale operation, preferring to wait until the Hungarians consented to a total removal of the country's Jews.[7] The occupation provided that opportunity.

It turned out that the Nazis found in Hungary a group of accomplices who outdid even them in their eagerness to eliminate the Jews from the country. And indeed, it was primarily the joint, concerted, and single-minded drive by these two groups that made the effectuation of the Final Solution in Hungary possible: neither group could have succeeded without the other. While the Germans were eager to solve the Jewish question, they could not take action without the consent of the newly established Hungarian puppet government and the cooperation of the Hungarian instruments of power. And the Hungarian ultra-rightists, though anxious to emulate their German counterparts, could not have achieved their ideologically defined objectives in the absence of the German occupation.

As a consequence of the occupation the Hungarian Jewish community, which had survived the first four and a half years of the war relatively intact, was subjected to the most ruthless and concentrated destruction process of the Nazis' war against the Jews. The drive against the Hungarian Jews took place on the very eve of Allied victory, when the grisly details of the Final Solution were already known to the leaders of the world, including those of Hungarian and world Jewry. Informed about the barbarity and speed with which the Hungarian Jews were liquidated, Winston Churchill concluded that it was "probably the greatest and most horrible crime ever committed in the history of the world."[8]

The liquidation of Hungarian Jewry reminds one of a prophecy by Theodore Herzl. In a letter dated March 10, 1903, when Hungarian Jewry was still in the midst of its Golden Era, the father of Zionism cautioned his friend Ernö Mezei, a member of the Hungarian Parliament: "The hand of fate shall also seize Hungarian Jewry. And the later this occurs, and the stronger this Jewry becomes, the more cruel and hard shall be the blow, which shall be delivered with greater savagery. There is no escape."

Was there no escape? The evidence clearly indicates that had Horthy and the clique around him *really* wanted to save Hungarian Jewry they could have done so. According to the testimony of Veesenmayer and Otto Winkelmann, the former Higher SS and Police Leader in Hungary, in the postwar trial of Andor Jaross, László Baky, and László Endre—the triumvirate primarily responsible for the destruction of Hungarian Jewry—the Final Solution of the Jewish question was only a *wish*, not an absolute *demand* of the Germans. The Eichmann-*Sonderkommando*, numbering less than 200, could not possibly have carried out its sinister plans without the wholehearted cooperation of the Hungarians who placed the instruments of state power at its disposal. As the example of Bulgaria, Finland, and Romania reveals—and Horthy's own actions of July 1944 clearly indicate—the Regent and his associates could have saved most of the Jews. Unfortunately, they were interested primarily in protecting the assimilated ones, especially those with whom they had good and mutually advantageous business and financial relations; they were almost as eager as the Right radicals to rid the country of the "Eastern-Galician" Jews. It was partially for this reason that Horthy, who considered the imminent Nazi occupation less of an evil than a possible Soviet invasion, had made certain concessions that proved fatal for Hungarian Jewry. Meeting Hitler at Schloss Klessheim the day before the occupation, he had consented to "the delivery of a few hundred thousand Jewish workers to Germany for employment in war-related projects."[9] Apparently Horthy was convinced that by giving this consent he would not only satisfy Germany's "legitimate" needs, but also contribute to the struggle against Bolshevism and at the same time get rid of the Galician Jews, whom he openly detested. The Eichmann-*Sonderkommando* and its Hungarian accomplices took full advantage of this agreement to implement the Final Solution program throughout the country, based on the argument that "the Jews will be more productive in Germany if they have all members of their families with them."

Once they were given the green light, the dejewification experts proceeded with lightning speed. Time was of the essence, for the Third Reich was threatened by imminent defeat. And, indeed, in no other country was the Final Solution program—the establishment of the central and local Jewish Councils, the isolation, expropriation, ghettoization, concentration, entrainment, and deportation of the Jews—carried out with as much barbarity and speed as in Hungary. Although the dejewification squads were relatively small, the interplay of many domestic and international factors aided them in the speedy implementation of their sinister designs.

The German and Hungarian agents in charge of the Final Solution program had at their disposal the instruments of state power—the police, gendarmerie, and civil service—and were able to proceed unhindered by any internal or external opposition. The puppet government provided them with "legal" and administrative cover, and a considerable number of Hungarians proved eager and willing to collaborate for ideological or materialistic reasons. With public opinion having been successfully molded by years of vicious anti-Semitic agitation, the population at large was at best passive; the bulk of the "proletariat," including the miners and industrial workers, continued the political stance of the 1930's, embracing the Arrow Cross rather than the leftist parties.

The Passivity of the Non-Jewish World

Postwar Hungarian historiography notwithstanding, there was no meaningful resistance anywhere in the country, let alone organized opposition for the protection of the Jews. This was especially so in the countryside. It was primarily in Budapest that Christians and a variety of Church organizations were ready to offer shelter to Jews, saving thousands of them from certain death. But by that time late in 1944, the countryside was already *Judenrein*, the Soviet forces were fast approaching the capital, and most Hungarians realized that the Allies were bound to win the war.

The Allies, though fully aware of the realities of the Final Solution, were reluctant to get involved in the Nazis' war against the Jews. When the Western Powers were asked, shortly after the beginning of the deportations from Hungary on May 15, 1944, to bomb Auschwitz and the rail lines leading to the camp they declined, stating among other things that they could not spare aircraft for such "secondary targets." (A few months later, by contrast, they assembled a large armada to destroy another target without real strategic value: Dresden, the art-laden city.) The Soviet air force, which was strategically in even better position to bomb the death camps and the rail lines leading to them, also did nothing about them. The record of the leftist, mostly pro-Soviet, underground and partisan forces in Hungary, Slovakia and Poland is no better in this regard. There is no evidence that they engaged in any but the most isolated individual acts of sabotage or resistance to prevent the deportation of the Jews.

During the first phase of the deportations from Hungary, the attitude of the neutral states—Portugal, Turkey, Spain, Sweden, and Switzerland—was fundamentally no more positive. But their position, like that of the Vatican and the International Red Cross, changed when late in June 1944 the Swiss press began to publicize the horrors of the Final Solution in Hungary. Their pressure on Horthy, complementing his concerns over the rapidly deteriorating military situation—by that time the Soviet forces were fast approaching the borders of Hungary and the Western Allies had successfully established their beachheads in Normandy—advanced the desired result. Horthy halted the deportations on July 7. (In fact, the dejewification squads continued their operations around Budapest up to July 9.) By that date, all of Hungary with the exception of Budapest had been made *Judenrein*. The success of Horthy's belated action is another piece of evidence demonstrating that the German demands for the Final Solution could have been refused or sabotaged even after the occupation. Had Horthy and the Hungarian authorities really been concerned with all their citizens of the Jewish faith, they could have refused to cooperate. Without the Hungarian instruments of state power, the Germans would have been as helpless during the first phase of the occupation as they proved to be after early July 1944. Moreover, had Horthy decided not to continue as head of state after the occupation, depriving the Quisling government of legitimacy, perhaps even the police, gendarmerie, and the civil service would have been less enthusiastic in serving the Germans and their Hungarian accomplices.[10]

What about the victims, the Jewish masses and their leaders? Though the German invasion of Hungary took place on the eve of Allied victory, when the Hungarian and Jewish leaders were already privy to the secrets of Auschwitz, the ghettoization and deportation process in Hungary was carried out as smoothly as it was almost everywhere else in Nazi-dominated Europe. Helpless and defenseless, abandoned by the Christian society surrounding them, the Jews of Hungary—with the notable exception of some young Zionist pioneers in Budapest—displayed little or no opposition throughout the occupation period. In accordance with well-tested Nazi camouflage methods, the Jews were lulled into acquiescence by assurances that the deportations involved merely their relocation for labor within the country and Germany for the duration of the war. They—and the rest of the world—were further assured that the young and the old were included in the transports only out of "consideration for the close family-life pattern of the Jews."

Under the conditions of relative normality that prevailed until the German occupation, the predominantly assimilated leaders of Hungarian Jewry were quite effective in serving the community. Firmly committed to the values and principles of the traditional conservative-aristocratic system and convinced that the interests of Jewry were intimately intertwined with those of the Magyars, they never contemplated the use of independent political techniques for the advancement of Jewish interests per se. They took pride in calling themselves "Magyars of the Jewish faith" (*Zsidóvallású magyarok*). The leadership, consisting primarily of patriotic, rich, and generally conservative elements, tried to maintain the established order by faithfully obeying the commands of the government and fully associating itself with the values, beliefs, and interests of the broader Hungarian society. Consequently, the national Jewish leaders' response to the exacerbating anti-Jewish measures during the interwar period was apologetic and isolated from the general struggle of European Jewry. Their loyalty to the Hungarian nation, and their attachment to the gentry-aristocratic establishment, remained unshaken. To the end, they followed an ostrich-like policy, hoping against hope that the ruling elite would protect them from the fate of the Jewish communities of the neighboring countries.

As proven by the consequences of the German occupation, the Jews' display of patriotism failed to protect them from the "exterminationist" anti-Semitism of the Nazis. As Victor Karady, the well-known sociologist observed:

> [The Jews' display of assimilated status "worked" only] in a hypothetical way, as a belief in or a hope for such protection, much like wishful thinking or self-fulfilling prophesies. The argument ran that the more Jews kept up their ostensible attachment to Magyardom the more they would be preserved from the worst. Jewish community leadership professed this self-convincing ideology to the end and even collaborated with the Nazi authorities on the strength of this conviction. They thought that it would at least give them a strong moral standing with the Hungarian authorities, a capital potentially convertible into protection. "Jewish Hungarians stick to Magyardom even in the face of their undeserved persecution."... The continuation of assimilationist attitudes to the very end also made it easier for the community leadership as well as many other Jews to save face and justify their earlier assimilationist commitments.[11]

Of course, neither the Jewish leaders nor the Jewish masses envisioned the possibility that Germany would invade an ally and that the anti-Nazi Christian leadership would also be among the first victims after an occupation. Practically until the beginning of the deportations, the national Jewish leadership continued to believe that the Hungarian Jewish community, unlike all other large European Jewish communities, would emerge from the war relatively intact even if economically generally ruined. While tragically mistaken, their belief that they would escape the Holocaust—*megusszuk* (we'll get by), they frequently said in self-assurance—was not irrational. After all, Hungary had in fact been an island of safety in an ocean of destruction for four and a half years of the war.

The Jewish leaders' faith in the Hungarian establishment was not entirely groundless. They personally along with close to 150,000 of the 247,000 Jews of Budapest (including some 62,000 converts identified as Jews in 1941) were spared the fate that befell those in the countryside because Horthy, under great diplomatic and military pressure, halted the deportations early in July 1944. In addition, many tens of thousands of Jewish males of military age from all parts of Hungary were saved by the armed forces.

This represents still another paradox of the Holocaust in Hungary. The Hungarian labor service system, which was unique in Nazi-dominated Europe, had been the major source of Jewish suffering before the German occupation. Deprived of their dignity and rights, the Jewish labor servicemen were compelled to do hard and often hazardous military-related work under the constant prodding of mostly cruel guards and officers. Particularly tragic was the fate of the tens of thousands of labor servicemen who had been deployed, along with the Second Hungarian Army, on the Soviet front and in the copper mines in Bor, Serbia. Yet, after the occupation, the Jewish labor servicemen—unlike the Jews at large who at first were placed under the jurisdiction of the Germans—enjoyed the continued protection of the Hungarian armed forces. Moreover, many Jewish males were recruited by decent military commanders from the ghettos and concentration centers, saving them from deportation and almost certain death.[12]

Postwar Reactions

As elsewhere in the former Nazi-dominated world, in Hungary too the Holocaust became a highly controversial issue after the war. The subject of much public debate during the first postwar years, largely because of the revelations of the war crimes trials, the Holocaust gradually declined as a major public issue and emerged as a very uncomfortable chapter in postwar Hungarian history. Relatively few Christians—whether politicians, professionals, or laypersons—managed to come to grips with it honestly either during or after the Communist era.

During the Communist era (1949-1989) the Holocaust, like the Jewish question as a whole, was gradually submerged in the Orwellian memory hole of history, although in a more restrained fashion than in the other Soviet-bloc nations. While the Communists never denied the horrendous crimes committed by the Nazis, they systematically ignored or distorted the Holocaust by routinely subsuming the losses of Jewry as losses incurred by their own nations.

During the post-Communist era, the treatment of the Holocaust has varied all across the newly evolved political spectrum. On the extreme Right are the historical revisionists, the charlatans from the lunatic fringes of Hungarian society who specialize in the distortion and outright denial of the Holocaust. Like their counterparts elsewhere, they are engaged in an obscene campaign to absolve the Nazis and their Hungarian accomplices of all crimes committed against the Jews. They are involved in a sinister drive to destroy the historical record—and memory—and make the world forget the consequences of the Nazis' war against the Jews. Among them are anti-Semites who are committed to the Nazi thesis identifying Bolshevism with Jewry. In their reckoning, the suffering of the Jews during the war is more than balanced by the "even greater suffering" Jews inflicted on their nation through Communism.

The failure to come to grips with the Holocaust is also manifested in less extreme and more benign forms. Many highly respectable individuals acknowledge the mass murder of the Jews, but place exclusive blame on the Germans. Others attempt to generalize the Holocaust by lumping the losses of Jewry with those incurred by the military. Still others, including top officials of the government, would like to close the book on World War II and ease their conscience by honoring all casualties, blurring the fundamental differences between persons who were murdered on racial grounds without regard to age or sex and those who—without minimizing their tragedy—fell as a consequence of hostilities in an aggressive war on the side of the Axis. There are others in this group who try to mitigate the impact of the Holocaust by comparing, if not identifying, the horrors of Nazism with those of Communism and by rationalizing the Hungarian involvement by citing the impact of the "injustices" of Trianon. And finally there are those who try to ease their conscience by emphasizing the number of Jews who were saved in Hungary. In their drive to rehabilitate Miklós Horthy—and by implication the entire Horthy era—these cleansers of history attribute the survival of the Jews of Budapest exclusively to the Regent's decision of July 7, 1944 to halt the deportations. Eager to assure Hungary's historical continuity as a "chivalrous" nation, these nationalists fail to acknowledge the important role that others played. In the post-Communist era it has become politically fashionable and historically prudent not to mention the determining role the Red Army played in the liberation of the surviving Jews of Hungary, including those of Budapest.

These negative manifestations notwithstanding, post-Communist Hungary has made considerable progress toward coming to grips with the tragedy of its Jewish community. It decided to make some reparation to the surviving remnant of Hungarian Jewry and passed a law on the rights of ethnic and national minorities. But while the Hungarian government has been forceful in condemning anti-Semitism and eloquent in paying tribute to the victims of the Holocaust, it failed so far at least to make a national, collective commitment to confront the Holocaust honestly and truthfully.[13]

NOTES

1. See his *The Dissolution of the Habsburg Monarchy* (Chicago: University of Chicago Press, 1929), p. 825. See also Randolph L. Braham, *The Politics of Genocide. The Holocaust in Hungary* (New York: Columbia University Press, 1994), pp. 5-12. (Cited hereafter as Braham, *Politics*.)

2. For some details on the Golden Era, see *ibid.*, pp. 1-39.

3. Jenö Lévai, *Zsidósors Magyarországon* (Jewish Fate in Hungary) (Budapest: Magyar Téka, 1948), p. 17.

4. Braham, *Politics*, pp. 129-30.

5. For details on the pre-occupation losses of Hungarian Jewry, see *ibid.*, pp. 205-22.

6. "Edmund Veesenmayer's Memorandum to the German Foreign Office dated December 10, 1943" in *The Destruction of Hungarian Jewry. A Documentary Account*, Randolph L. Braham, comp. and ed. (New York: World Federation of Hungarian Jews, 1973), pp. 254-84.

7. Braham, *Politics*, pp. 283-93.

8. For details on the Final Solution program in Hungary, see *ibid.*, chapters 17-22.

9. *Ibid.*, pp. 391, 397-401. See also C.A. Macartney, *October Fifteenth. A History of Modern Hungary* (Edinburgh: Edinburgh University Press, 1997), Vol. 2, pp. 234, 239.

10. For details on the reaction of the Allies, the neutral states, the Vatican, and the International Red Cross, see Braham, *Politics*, pp. 1205-94.

11. See his "Identity Strategies Under Duress Before and After the Shoah" in *The Holocaust in Hungary. Fifty Years Later*, Randolph L. Braham and Attila Pók, eds. (New York: Columbia University Press, 1997), p. 157.

12. For details on all aspects of the labor service system, see Braham, *Politics*, pp. 294-380.

13. For details, see *ibid.*, chapter 33.

2

What Did They Know and When?

In the agonizing debate over the activities of the leaders of the doomed wartime Jewish communities, the behavior of the Hungarian Jewish leadership has come under special scrutiny. Hungarian Jewry managed to survive largely unharmed until the second quarter of 1944, when many of the "secrets of Auschwitz" had already surfaced and the downfall of the Third Reich was generally considered inevitable. Yet when the mass deportations of Hungarian Jews began on May 15, 1944:

— The "provincial" Jews (those living outside Budapest) were destroyed at an unprecedented speed in the most ruthless deportation and massacre program of the war.

— These Jews behaved in a resigned and docile manner throughout the ghettoization, concentration, and deportation processes.

— The deportation of the Jews of Budapest, the last surviving community, was halted on July 7, 1944 by Admiral Miklós Horthy, the regent of Hungary, after he had been approached, *inter alia,* by the king of Sweden, the Vatican, and his own son, Miklós Horthy, Jr., who had been informed about the realities of Auschwitz by the national Hungarian Jewish leaders some time in June.

These facts, which are generally recognized, give rise to a number of controversial and bewildering questions. What exactly did the national leaders of Hungarian Jewry in Budapest know about the extermination of the Jews in Nazi-occupied Europe and when did they acquire this knowledge? If they were aware of the Nazi program for the "Final Solution of the Jewish Question in Europe," why did they not inform the Jewish masses—or at least the leaders of the provincial

---

Reprinted from *The Holocaust as Historical Experience*, Yehuda Bauer and Nathan Rotenstreich, eds. (New York: Holms & Meier, 1981) with permission of the publisher.

Jewish communities—in time? Why did they fail to enlighten Hungarian public opinion and why did they not inform Horthy and the other governmental leaders of Hungary until the second half of June when the bulk of the provincial Jews had already been deported? These are the questions that arose most conspicuously in the postwar controversy over Rezsö Kasztner (Rudolph Kastner).[1]

Currently available evidence indicates that many, if not all, of the national leaders of Hungarian Jewry were fully aware of the progress of the Final Solution in Nazi-occupied Europe well before the German occupation of Hungary. Although their information about the mass extermination of the Jews was perhaps not totally substantiated during the first two years of the war,[2] the hard-core evidence was fully at hand weeks before the beginning of the mass deportations from Hungary.

The sources of information of Jewish leaders were many and varied. They included:

— Newscasts by "enemy" radio stations including the BBC, the Voice of America, and "Kossuth Radio," the Hungarian-language transmissions from Moscow;

— "Illegal" contacts with Jewish organizations abroad, especially the Zionist and Orthodox units in Switzerland, Palestine, Istanbul, and Bratislava;

— Refugees and camp escapees from Poland, Slovakia, and elsewhere;

— Reports by Hungarian soldiers and officers;

— Contacts with German military, police, and intelligence officers, including those affiliated with the *Wehrmacht,* the SS, and the *Abwehr.*

The First Revelations about the Mass Murders

Although the details of the "Final Solution of the Jewish Question in Europe" were discussed only at the Wannsee Conference on January 20, 1942, the mass execution of Jews had begun soon after the invasion of the Soviet Union on June 22, 1941. Hundreds of thousands of Polish and Soviet Jews had been systematically rounded up and shot by the *SS-Einsatzgruppen,* the mobile killing units that followed the Nazi armies, before the extermination camps were set up in Poland.[3] Among these were also the 14,000 to 16,000 "alien" Jews who had been deported from Hungary in August 1941. Their liquidation near Kamenets Podolsk was, in fact, the first five-figure massacre of the Holocaust period.[4]

In spite of the stringent security measures taken by the SS, the killings were too massive to be totally concealed either from the local population or from members of the Nazi satellite armies, including the Romanians and the Hungarians. Numerous Hungarian soldiers, appalled by the machine-gunning of innocent men, women, and children, expressed shock in letters to their families, giving detailed reports when home on furlough. Many of these accounts were brought to the attention of the Jewish leaders and some of them were even reported in the American press.[5] Such accounts were also fully corroborated by those escapees who managed to return to Hungary. One of the survivors, by the name of Stern, accompanied by a delegation from the *Magyar Izraeliták Pártfogó Irodája* (Welfare Bureau of Hungarian Jews) led by György Polgár, gave details of the massacres at Kamenets Podolsk to Ferenc Keresztes-Fischer, the Minister of the Interior. The latter was visibly shocked and ordered a halt to all further deportations.[6]

The first public disclosure relating to the mass killings of Jews was made by Thomas Mann, the noted novelist, in his BBC broadcasts of December 1941 and January 1942.[7] Soon afterwards, Slovak escapees from camps in the area of Poland under the "General Government" (*General gouvernement*) confirmed that Jews were being massacred in them. The first of many transports of Slovakian Jews left from Poprad for Auschwitz on March 26, 1942; by the end of April a few escapees managed to return and provide the earliest evidence about the fate of the deportees. Their accounts were forwarded by the *Ustredna Zidov* (Central Jewish Office), the Nazi-established central "authority" representing the Jews of Slovakia, to Jewish organizations in Britain, Palestine, and Switzerland as well as to the leaders of the Slovakian state, including President Josef Tiso.

The Vatican was apparently also aware of the realities in Poland by this date. During the first wave of deportations from Slovakia, the Papal Nuncio in Bratislava, Msgr. Giuseppe Burzio, informed Tiso and his Prime Minister Vojtech Tuka that the Jews were being gassed and pleaded for the ending of the deportations. In response to this intervention, Tuka asked Dieter Wisliceny at the German legation, who had been organizing the deportations, for permission to send a Slovak delegation to inspect the situation of the deportees (June 1942). Wisliceny denied the "rumor" of the gassing, but adopted dilatory tactics concerning the request. At the same time he alerted Berlin and recommended that, in the interest of continued good German-Slovak relations, the deportations be halted. By that time about 55,000 Jews, or two-thirds of the Slovak Jewish community, had already been deported.[8]

In May 1942 the Jewish Socialist party of Poland, the "Bund," transmitted a detailed report to London informing the world that the Germans had "embarked on the physical extermination of the Jewish population on Polish soil." The report was broadcast over the BBC on June 2 and 26, 1942; details were also published by the *Daily Telegraph* on June 25 as well as by the Jewish press. However, the world at large remained complacent. Jewish leaders in the free world "made no visible attempt to put pressure on their governments for any active policy of rescue."[9]

Late in July 1942, representatives of some of the leading Jewish organizations in neutral Switzerland received firsthand information about the resolution of the Nazi hierarchy to bring about the physical liquidation of European Jewry in the course of the war. There has been, however, a certain lack of clarity as to how the information reached them.

According to Arthur D. Morse's account, Gerhart Riegner, the representative of the World Jewish Congress in Switzerland, was informed on August 1, 1942 by a leading German industrialist who had access to Hitler's headquarters, that the *Führer* had ordered the extermination of the Jews of Europe. The informant had overheard a discussion of the order, which also stipulated the use of prussic acid, the lethal ingredient of the Zyklon B gas that was actually used in the extermination camps. By that time, presumably, Riegner was already aware of the Bund report and had information about the "resettlement" of 380,000 Jews in the Warsaw Ghetto, which had begun on July 22, and about the deportation of Jews from occupied Belgium, Holland and France.

Because of wartime censorship regulations, and in order to assure privacy, Riegner forwarded his report in the form of a telegram through the American Consulate in Geneva on August 8. Vice-Consul Howard Etling, Jr. included a covering memorandum to the State Department in which he evaluated Riegner as "a serious and balanced individual," requesting that the message be delivered to Rabbi Stephen S. Wise, head of the World Jewish Congress. The telegram was at first suppressed by the State Department, but when it was discovered that the British Foreign Office had forwarded its copy to the London branch of the World Jewish Congress, Rabbi Wise was finally notified on August 28.

According to evidence now available, however, the real source of Riegner's information was a fiercely anti-Nazi officer, Lt. Col. Artur Sommer.* A highly esteemed economist, Sommer had been attached early in the war to the Wehrmacht High Command. In this capacity, and as a member of a German economic delegation, he often visited Switzerland officially and ostensibly for the advancement of German economic interests. An anti-Nazi who opposed Hitler's war, Sommer reestablished and maintained discreet contact with Professor Edgar Salin of Basel University, his former teacher. Sommer became the conduit of invaluable information for the Allies. It was Sommer, for example, who tipped off Stalin some time in June 1941 about the Nazis' plan for the imminent attack on the Soviet Union.

Appalled by the Nazis' design to exterminate the Jews, Sommer revealed the information to Stalin with the following request that it be relayed to Churchill and Roosevelt:[10]

> In the East, camps are being prepared where all the Jews of Europe and a great part of the Russian prisoners of war will be exterminated by gas. Please relay this information immediately to Churchill and Roosevelt personally. If the BBC comes out every day with a warning against lighting the gas ovens, then perhaps they may not be put into

* The real informant, it turned out, was a businessman named Eduard Schulte. See Walter Laqueur and Richard Breitman, *Breaking the Silence* (New York: Simon and Schuster, 1986), 320 p.

> operation, for the criminals are doing everything to prevent the German people from finding out what they are planning to do and will certainly carry out.

Salin passed on the information received from Sommer to another former student of his, Dr. Chaim Pozner, co-director of the Palestine Office in Switzerland. Pozner gave the information immediately to V. C. Farrell, head of the British Passport Control Office in Geneva, who also served as the center of British Intelligence in Switzerland. Concurrently, Dr. Pozner informed Dr. Benjamin Sagalowitz, director of the press bureau of the Union of Jewish Communities in Switzerland, who in turn alerted Riegner.[11]

In addition to the information received from Sagalowitz, Riegner continued to submit corroborative documentation concerning Hitler's resolution to "solve" the Jewish question. But this, like all subsequent communications by Riegner and others, remained for a long time unheeded.

In desperation (months after receiving Riegner's first information), Rabbi Wise contacted President Roosevelt on December 2, 1942 and again on December 8, when he also submitted a 20-page document titled *Blueprint for Extermination* in which he presented a country-by-country analysis of the extermination program. The Allies were reluctant to diminish their general war effort for any overt rescue scheme in behalf of the Jews, arguing that an Allied victory offered the only remedy for the Jews' plight. The Jewish leaders in the West, on the other hand, apparently feared that by pressing for direct action to rescue European Jewry their own patriotism might be impugned.

Having rejected suggestions for an overt and direct rescue operation as incompatible with their war aims, the Allies nevertheless agreed to issue a joint statement on December 17, 1942, in which they condemned the Nazi extermination of the Jews. The conspiracy of silence was at last broken. From then on, Allied broadcasts aimed at the world at large contained more specific information about Nazi exterminations of the Jews.

The Revelations by Polish and Slovak Refugees

The Hungarian Jewish leaders were particularly well placed to ascertain the veracity of the foreign radio broadcasts, since thousands of Jewish refugees had escaped into Hungary from Poland and Slovakia in the wake of anti-Jewish measures. Some had been smuggled into Hungary with the assistance of the Budapest Relief and Rescue Committee, which was organized by the Zionists, including Kasztner, Ottó Komoly, and Joel Brand.[12] The latter was in charge of the *Tiyul* section, dealing with underground "human smuggling" operations. One of the major functions of the Rescue Committee was to collect and transmit the personal accounts of the escapees to its Jewish Agency contacts in Istanbul and Switzerland. The Budapest office set up a regular underground intelligence unit, where escapees were closely questioned and details about the ghettoization, concentration, and extermination program in Poland and Slovakia carefully scrutinized and counterchecked. It has been claimed that hundreds of such accounts were thus authenticated in Budapest and forwarded to the Rescue Committee offices in Istanbul and Switzerland.[13]

Reports of this nature were also collected and forwarded to the Jewish Agency offices in Istanbul and Switzerland by Gisi Fleischmann of the Rescue Committee of Bratislava.[14] She also kept the Hungarian Jewish leaders, especially those associated with the Kasztner group, abreast of developments in Poland and Slovakia on a regular basis.[15] Moreover, members of the Bratislava and Budapest Rescue Committees exchanged visits periodically. In addition, the Orthodox leadership of Hungarian Jewry was also informed separately by Rabbi Michael Dov Weissmandel of the Bratislava Committee.

The Bratislava Rescue Committee, for example, reported to the Budapest Committee, some weeks before the beginning of the Hungarian deportations in May 1944, that a railways agreement had been signed between Hungary and Slovakia and that the SS were in the process of improving and renovating the gas chambers and crematoria in Auschwitz in anticipation of the imminent arrival of the Hungarian Jews.[16] The report even quoted the words of a *Scharführer* that the SS "will soon eat fine Hungarian salami."[17]

It was Gisi Fleischmann who had established contact with Wisliceny on May 7, 1943, for the negotiation of the so-called "Europa Plan" for rescuing the Jews of Europe.[18] She was then already reporting to Jewish Agency offices in Istanbul and

Switzerland; for instance, on March 24, 1943 she had identified the three major centers where Jews were still in existence as Auschwitz, Birkenau, and Lublin, emphasizing that those still alive were basically healthy men and women able to work.[19] On May 9 she reported further that even those selected for work in the camps were liable to be murdered there. "As long as the individual continues to be capable of working he justifies his right to exist. Should he become weak, or prevented by illness from carrying out his work, he simply ceases to exist."[20]

On May 10 (a few days after her meeting with Wisliceny), Gisi Fleischmann communicated not only the conditions worked out by Wisliceny and his "superiors" for the effectuation of the "Europa Plan," but also further details about the annihilation of the Jews in Poland. She wrote, *inter alia:*

> We are under the spell of the *schlichim* [couriers], who brought us reports that make the blood run cold. Over one million *chaverim* [comrades] have already been resettled from *Ziwiah* [Poland], the location is unknown. Hundreds of thousands more lost their life due to starvation, disease and cold, and uncounted others, numbering many many tens of thousands, have fallen victim to violence. The reports state that the corpses are used as chemical raw materials. The reports also agree with the news of some *plitim* [refugees] who were fortunate enough to escape in the most daring ways. We have also received written reports to the same effect from the *schlichim.* Into a cattle wagon which would normally hold 40 are crammed 120 *chaverim.* There is a layer approximately 10 centimeters deep of unslaked lime on the floor, and since the people in the wagons must relieve themselves where they are standing, when the wastes touch the lime, gases are formed which bring about an exceedingly high mortality rate. It is presumed that those who were resettled from *Ziwiah* are being taken beyond the Bug, but so far no sign of life has reached us from there.[21]

The communications by Gisi Fleischmann, like those of the Budapest Rescue Committee,[22] constitute some of the most convincing evidence that Jewish leaders in various parts of the world, including, of course, Hungary, were fully acquainted with the Nazi massacre program.

Among Jewish refugees in Hungary, some were partisans who had been captured but had managed to escape, acquire Aryan papers, and live semi-legally in the country. One of these was Bruce B.

Teicholz who, after capture north of Munkács, was brought to Hungary in March 1942. He managed to escape in Budapest and joined a Polish-Jewish underground organization under the code name "Glick." Under the name of Bronislaw Szczepipiorka, he was registered as a Polish Christian with the *Külföldieket Elienörzö Országos Kózponti Hatoság* (National Central Alien Control Office), the agency entrusted with jurisdiction over foreign nationals living in Hungary. In this triple capacity Teicholz maintained close contact with the Polish refugee organizations in Hungary and abroad, with Dr. A. Silberschein of the World Jewish Congress in Geneva, with the official leaders of Hungarian Jewry, including Samu Stern and Fülöp (Philipp de) Freudiger, and with the members of the Budapest Rescue Committee, including Kasztner, Komoly and Brand.

Teicholz claims that at some time in April 1943 he had a meeting with the leaders of Hungarian Jewry, including Freudiger, Kasztner, Moshe (Miklós) Krausz of the Palestine Office, and Dr. József Pásztor of the *Országos Magyar Zsidó Segitö Akció* (National Hungarian Jewish Assistance Campaign), the major Jewish fund-raising organization. At this meeting he claims to have explained in detail the techniques employed by the Germans in pursuing the Final Solution in Poland. He further claims to have reviewed the techniques used to lull Jews into submission and cooperation in their own destruction, and warned the Hungarian Jewish leaders to take all necessary precautionary measures. These leaders "assured" Teicholz that what was happening in Poland could not possibly happen in Hungary.

Teicholz's account is also corroborated by that of Hermann Adler, the German-Jewish poet and author, who fled to Budapest in October 1943 after having spent the previous two years in the underground movement in the Vilna, Bialystok, and Warsaw Ghettos. As a member of the underground in Poland, Adler was also in touch with Anton Schmidt, the by now legendary German army sergeant, and a number of other Germans involved in the anti-Nazi resistance, among them Franz Fritsch. By the time of his arrival in Budapest, Adler was fully familiar with the extermination of the Jews at Treblinka and the realities of the Final Solution program in Poland as a whole. He revealed all he knew to Professor Valdemar Langlet, the representative of the Swedish Red Cross in Budapest, and to the leaders of Hungarian Jewry, including those associated with the

Budapest Rescue Committee. These leaders, Adler claims, refused to believe his accounts about Treblinka. Kasztner, for example, wanted to know whether he (Adler) was in Treblinka personally and whether he was speaking from personal experience. "It wasn't easy to convince the Hungarian Jews," Adler complained.[23]

Acknowledgements by Jewish Leaders

Hungarian Jewish leaders have since admitted that they knew the facts about the camps, facts such as those revealed by Teicholz and Adler. Describing the circumstances under which he had emerged as head of the Jewish Council of Budapest, the agency entrusted with "power" over all of Hungarian Jewry, Samu Stern wrote:

> The good-will faking, hypocritical and treacherous debut of the Gestapo did not take me in, nor others, I suppose; I knew what they had done in all German-occupied states of Europe.... I heard enough about the methods of the Gestapo's ill-famed Jewish department to know that they always shunned sensation, disliked creating panic and fear, worked noiselessly, coolly and in deepest secrecy, so that the listless, ignorant victims should be without an inkling of what was ahead of them even while the wagon was traveling with them toward death. I knew their habits, deeds and terrifying reputation, and yet I accepted the chairmanship of the Council. *And the others knew as much as I did when they entered the Council as members.*[24]

Kasztner was perhaps even better aware than Stern of the anti-Jewish measures throughout Europe, in view of his contacts with Jewish organizations abroad through various underground channels. In 1946 Kasztner issued a detailed report on the wartime activities of the Budapest Rescue Committee.[25] In it he provided both direct and indirect evidence that he and his colleagues on the Committee were fully aware of the anti-Jewish measures in Nazi-occupied Europe. While admitting this, however, he was basically silent about the failure to inform Hungarian Jewry, though all the more pugnacious and bitter over the passivity and complacency of the Jewish and non-Jewish leaders in the free world, who (he repeatedly insisted) had indeed been constantly supplied with ample information from Budapest.[26]

Appearing as a witness for the prosecution in the Veesenmayer Trial on March 19, 1948, Kasztner stated in answer to a question from Mr. Caming, one of the prosecutors: "We had, as early as 1942, a complete picture of what had been happening in the East with the Jews deported to Auschwitz and the other extermination camps."[27] Yet when he was asked by Dr. Doetzer, Veesenmayer's defense counsel, why Horthy had not been informed, Kasztner gave an evasive reply:

> We certainly should have tried this. We ought to have tried it, and we did, but you must visualize the situation in Hungary at the time immediately after the German occupation. It was a state of terror. Many of the friends and acquaintances through whom we could have informed Regent Horthy were already gone. Others were afraid to get in touch with us. It took quite some time before we had found the men and the opportunity to inform Horthy about it.[28]

While Kasztner was partially correct in depicting the situation after the German occupation, why were Horthy and other governmental leaders not informed *before* the occupation about what Kasztner's organization had known since 1942? This is particularly important in view of the power demonstrated by Horthy to halt the deportations in July 1944, allegedly after he had been enlightened about the exterminations.

During the trial of Malkiel Grünwald in 1954-1955 on a charge of having libeled Kasztner,[29] the latter testified:

> Toward the end of April 1944, the German military agents informed me that they had finally decided on the total deportation of Hungarian Jews.... An agreement was made between Hungary and Slovakia for the transfer of deportation trains from Hungary to Auschwitz.
>
> I also received information from Auschwitz that they were preparing there to receive the Hungarian Jews.... I was allowed by...Krumey to go to Kluj (Cluj, Kolozsvár) and contact... Wisliceny. This was approximately May 3, 1944.... A few days later I visited Wisliceny at his home in Budapest. He told me that it had finally been decided—total deportation.[30]

The visit of Kasztner to Kolozsvár, during the ghettoization of the Transylvanian Jews early in May 1944, has emerged as a major focus of the controversies surrounding the behavior of Jewish leaders during the Holocaust. Allegedly, Kasztner failed to inform the local Jewish Council and Rescue Committee leadership about the impending disaster. His closest friends there, including Hillel Danzig and Dezsö (David) Hermann, denied having been told anything about Auschwitz. Danzig made his denial at the Grünwald trial,[31] and Hermann in a taped interview with this writer (October 8, 1972).[32] It should be mentioned, however, that Hansi Brand, the wife of Joel Brand and herself a leading member of the Budapest Rescue Committee, was especially bitter about such details of knowledge by witnesses at the Grünwald trial when she in turn gave a taped interview (October 10, 1972). She claimed that the Jewish leaders in Kolozsvár were well aware of the impending threat.[33]

According to some of the witnesses summoned in Grünwald's defense, among them Jacob Freifeld and Yechiel Shmueli of Kolozsvár, several of the local Zionist leaders inadvertently supported the rumor planted by the Nazis that the Jews were being transferred to Kenyérmezö for labor[34] for the duration of the war.[35] Perhaps these leaders were as convinced about the genuineness of the plan as were most of the Jews deported from Northern Transylvania. But then the question is: Why did they decide to abandon the flock during a time of great peril? Instead of going with the masses to Kenyérmezö to provide continued leadership, most of them joined the group of 388 Jews taken to Budapest in accordance with the scheme agreed upon between Kasztner and the SS. From there they were removed on June 30, together with about 1,300 other "prominent Jews," to a special camp in Bergen Belsen and then eventually to Switzerland and freedom.[36]

Ernö Marton, the noted Zionist and former chief editor of the newspaper *Uj Kelet* (New East), escaped to Romania shortly after Kasztner's visit.[37] But the only "news" the Jewish masses received was that they would be transferred to work in Kenyérmezö or some other area in Transdanubia.

There are in fact clear indications that these leaders were informed by Kasztner about certain realities of the deportation of which the masses were kept in the dark. In response to a question by Judge Halevi, Kasztner confirmed that in Kolozsvár he had given his father-in-law Fischer certain hints and that "he had to know that there was deportation and that extermination would follow." When asked why the Jews of Kolozsvár did not know about all that, he confessed that his colleagues in Kolozsvár, including his father-in-law, "did not do all in their power—did not do all that could have been done—all that they had to do."[38]

The Auschwitz Protocols

The revelations by five Jewish escapees from Auschwitz in April-May 1944, just as the deportation of Hungarian Jews was getting under way, dispersed any doubts about the realities of the Nazis' "solution" of the Jewish question. While many attempted to flee the camp to save their own lives, these five escaped with the aid of the resistance movement to inform the world and warn the Jewish communities, especially in Hungary, about the impending disaster.[39]

The first to escape (on April 5, 1944) was Siegfried Lederer, whose mission was to alert the Jews in the Theresienstadt Ghetto and the International Red Cross in Geneva.[40] But by far the most important from the point of view of Hungarian Jewry was the escape of Walter Rosenberg (Rudolf Vrba)[41] and Alfred Wetzler (Josef Lanik)[42] on April 7. Both had enjoyed relatively special positions in the camp, enabling them to move freely throughout Auschwitz and collect exact information about the incoming transports and about the selection and extermination of the victims. On April 25, four days after reaching safety on Slovakian soil, they were telling their story at the Zilina headquarters of the Jewish Council to Dr. Oscar (Yermiyahu) Neumann, Oskar (Karmil) Krasznyansky and others. The escapees were closely scrutinized, their stories counterchecked and verified. The following day, after they had been interrogated anew, Krasznyansky prepared with the assistance of the escapees a detailed report in German.[43]

The report contained a detailed description of the camp, extensive data on the gassings, and sketches of the building plans, which were prepared by a professional architect. Krasznyansky's introduction to the report included biographical notes on the escapees and vouched for the accuracy and authenticity of their account.[44] He also added a supplement in which he urged the Allies to destroy the crematoria and the railroad lines leading to Auschwitz.[45] The so-called "working group" of the Jewish Community of Slovakia (including Gisi Fleischmann, Neumann, Weissmandel, and Krasznyansky himself) decided to forward the report to, *inter alia,* the Jewish Agency unit in Istanbul, Nathan Schwalb of the *chalutz* youth movement in Geneva, the Papal Nuncio in Bratislava, and Kasztner.[46]

The accounts of Vrba and Wetzler were fully corroborated a few weeks later by Arnost Rosin of Snina, Slovakia, and Czezlav Mordowicz of Mlawa, Poland, who escaped from Auschwitz on May 27 (i.e., shortly after the Hungarian deportations had begun). Their account, recorded by Krasznyansky during the first half of June 1944, provided data on the extermination of the Hungarian Jews up to the time of their flight.[47]

As to the exact date when the first set of Auschwitz Protocols (containing the testimony of Vrba and Lanik) were forwarded, the record is rather obscure. Vrba claims that he was assured by Krasznyansky and Neumann on April 26 that the report had already been sent to the Hungarians.[48] The memoirs of Neumann are vague about the dates,[49] but he has claimed that the Protocols were forwarded "shortly" after being typed.[50] Krasznyansky, on the other hand, claims that Kasztner, who visited Bratislava during those days, had read the original German text there and had him (Krasznyansky) translate the Protocols into Hungarian as well. He recalls that the Hungarian translation was forwarded to Budapest within two weeks.[51]

In his postwar report on the activities of the Rescue Committee of Budapest, Kasztner made absolutely no reference to the Auschwitz Protocols. They are also ignored by Samu Stern, who admits only to having received "in the middle of April" the news about a "railway conference" and the consequent allocation of "rolling stock for some unknown purpose."[52] Ernö Pető, one of the leading members of the Budapest Jewish Council, merely alludes to them in recounting how he tried some time in June to contact Andor Jaross, the Minister of the Interior, and Secretaries of State László Baky and László Endre, "to inform them personally of the already known horrors of Auschwitz." Unable to see any of the three, he managed to reveal his knowledge about Auschwitz to Lajos Reményi-Schneller, the Minister of Finance, and to the Nunciature.[53] Freudiger was also silent about them in "Report on Hungary," which he co-authored a few months after his arrival in Bucharest on August 10, 1944.[54] But later, in a taped interview with this author (October 10, 1972), Freudiger declared that he had received a copy of the Protocols from Weissmandel some time between June 5 and 10, 1944.[55]

While Krasznyansky and Kulka claim that Kasztner had taken along a copy of the Protocols from Bratislava in April 1944,[56] it appears that the "official" leaders of Hungarian Jewry learned about their content from Freudiger's copy. At the time that Freudiger admits having received the Protocols, the dejewification experts were already completing the deportations from Zone II (Transylvania) and beginning the concentration of the Jews in Zone III (Northern Hungary). But while German and Hungarian Nazis were pressing on with their program, Jewish leaders handled the Protocols "confidentially" in order "not to create panic"[57] and wasted invaluable time on translating them. In mid-June, Rabbi Fábián Herskovits was busy translating the Protocols from German into Italian with the assistance of Dr. Sára Friedländer and Lea Komoly Fürst, Ottó Komoly's daughter, "in order to transmit a copy to the Nuncio and the Pope."[58]

Only in late June did the Hungarian Jewish leaders begin to distribute copies of the Protocols among influential governmental and church leaders of Hungary and friends abroad. A copy was handed over by Pető to Miklós Horthy, Jr. for transmission to his father. On June 19 Miklós (Moshe) Krausz of the Palestine Office submitted an abbreviated English version of the protocols, together with a report on the ghettoization, concentration, and deportation processes in Zones I-III, to Switzerland on June 19, 1944, via Florian Manoliu, a member of the Romanian Legation in Berne. Krausz's material was duplicated and disseminated in Switzerland through the efforts of George (Mandel) Mantello, a Jewish businessman from the Transylvanian city of Beszterce, who was then serving as the First Secretary of the General Consulate of El Salvador in Geneva.[59] The credence of the material was enhanced through its distribution under a cover letter dated July 4, 1944, over the signatures of Professor Dr. Karl Barth of Basel, Professor Dr. Emil Brunner of Zürich, Dr. W.A. Visser t'Hooft of Geneva, and Pastor Vogt of Zürich.[60]

The Vatican, which was by that time well acquainted with the Nazi extermination program,[61] received the copy of the Vrba-Lanik Protocols that had been handed by the Bratislava Rescue Committee to Burzio late in April. However, the first overt reaction of the Vatican took place around June 20, presumably after it had also received the Rosin-Mordowicz Protocols. It was around this time that the Vatican's legate, a certain Monsignor Mario, arrived in Bratislava on a mission to interview the escapees from Auschwitz and double-check the veracity of their accounts. Krasznyansky consequently accompanied Vrba and Mordowicz to the Sváty Jur monastery near Bratislava, where they were interviewed in depth for five hours through the intermediation of a French interpreter.[62] Apparently the Papal legate was fully satisfied with the outcome of the interview, since the Pope addressed a personal plea to Horthy[63] on June 25, which was followed by the warning of President Roosevelt[64] on June 26, and by the intervention of King Gustav of Sweden[65] on June 30.

There is no doubt that these official, diplomatic interventions played an important (if not determining) role in Horthy's decision of July 7 to prohibit further deportations from Hungary. It is safe to assume, however, that had the first set of Protocols been publicized abroad and secretly distributed in Hungary almost immediately after their preparation, the deportations might have been interrupted significantly earlier. For although the BBC broadcast some sections from the Protocols, such broadcasts were construed by world public opinion basically as horror propaganda material. Had the Vatican and neutral countries, like Sweden and Switzerland, begun a vigorous press and radio campaign as soon as the Protocols were received from Bratislava, Horthy might have been induced to act earlier.

In fact, the Vatican and the neutrals were more concerned with maintaining strict neutrality than with publicizing their concern for the Jews of Hungary. The Swiss press began the campaign of attacking Hungary only during the second half of June, largely due to the initiatives taken by Mantello after he had received Krausz's material of June 19.[66] The Americans did not publicize the Protocols until November 1944, by which time the Nazis, faced with the advance of the Red Army, were already eager to demolish the extermination facilities and remove all traces of their crimes.[67]

Hungarian Governmental Awareness of the Catastrophe

Although the copy of the Protocols given by Pető to Miklós Horthy Jr. reached the Regent only in late June 1944,[68] there is ample evidence that he and many of the other leaders of Hungary were similarly well-acquainted with the Nazi anti-Jewish program long before the German occupation of the country. In April 1943, for example, during Horthy's first Schloss Klessheim meeting with Hitler, the latter recommended that Hungary should copy Poland, where "the Jews who did not want to work were simply shot." Ribbentrop added that the Jews "should either be killed or sent to concentration camps."[69] Upon his return to Hungary, Horthy drafted a letter defending himself and the Kállay Government against the reproach that Hungary had "failed to take as far-reaching an action in the extirpation of the Jews as Germany had taken or as would appear desirable in the other countries." This sentence, although not included in the final version of the letter (sent on May 7, 1943), clearly reveals that Horthy and the officials of the Ministry of Foreign Affairs who prepared the original draft had been informed about what was happening to the Jews of Germany.[70]

Döme Sztójay, Hungary's Minister in Berlin, who was to become Prime Minister after the German occupation, apparently knew about the Nazi design to "solve the Jewish question in a radical manner during the war" as early as 1942. He revealed his knowledge to György Ottlik, a member of the influential Foreign Affairs Committee of the Upper House of the Hungarian Parliament and the editor-in-chief of the German-language *Pester Lloyd* of Budapest, the semi-official organ of the Hungarian Government. Ottlik, who visited Germany in the course of his West European tour of August-September 1942, transmitted this information to the Hungarian Ministry of Foreign Affairs on October 10.[71] According to Dieter Wisliceny, "both Endre and Baky had been accurately informed as to what the deportations meant."[72] In his report of May 29. 1944, Lt.-Col. László Ferenczy, who had been in charge of the deportations, openly referred to Auschwitz as a place where the deported Jews were subjected to a process of "selection."[73]

The evidence now available indicates that even some of the anti-Nazi leaders in Hungary were acquainted with the Nazi extermination program. Kasztner claimed, though without providing sufficient evidence, that various leaders of the Social Democratic Party had been kept informed about the destruction of the European Jews and about the methods the Nazis had employed.[74] Angelo Rotta, the Apostolic Nuncio in Budapest, was also familiar with the realities of the deportations. In his letter of May 15, 1944, protesting the measures that the Hungarian Government was taking or planned to take against the Jews, the Nuncio remarked that "the whole world knows what the deportation means in practice."[75]

Questions and Arguments

The conclusion to be drawn from the foregoing is clear. Many of the Jewish and Christian leaders of the world, including of course the Hungarian ones, possessed well-substantiated knowledge about the extermination program since the spring of 1942 and irrefutable evidence since April 1944. Nonetheless, the deportations that began in Hungary on May 15 were not halted until July 7, when only the Jews of Budapest remained.

It is almost universally supposed that Horthy decided to halt the deportations in response to the interventions made by foreign state and church leaders, who were motivated to act, *inter alia*, by the Auschwitz Protocols. The interventions were presumably reinforced by Horthy's own reaction to the Protocols, which had been shown to him by his son during the second half of June. Yet these assumptions give rise to a number of bewildering questions. Why were the first Protocols not forwarded to those world leaders soon after their completion on April 26? Why were the provincial Hungarian Jewish leaders and masses not alerted to their content? What would have been the result of alerting them before the deportations began?

These questions are obviously controversial and require a careful differentiation among facts, claims, and presumptions. The established *facts* include the following:

- The escapees from Auschwitz told their story to the Jewish leaders of Slovakia on April 25 and 26, 1944.
- Freudiger admitted to having received the Protocols between June 5-10.

— Kasztner admitted having known of the mass destruction of the Jews in Nazi-occupied Europe before the German occupation of Hungary.

— The Hungarian Jewish masses were not authoritatively informed about them.

— The deportation of the Jews from Carpatho-Ruthenia and Transylvania (Zones I and II) began on May 15 and was completed on June 7, and the deportation of the Jews of Northern Hungary (Zone III) did not begin until June 11.

— The Hungarian Jewish leaders were still busy translating and duplicating the Protocols on June 14-16 and distributed them only later in June.

— The Hungarian Jewish leaders completely ignored the Protocols in their postwar memoirs and statements.

Although the *claims* advanced in connection with the Protocols are both plausible and to a considerable extent convincing, there is no conclusive evidence to substantiate them. Among the claims are:

— The contention of Krasznyansky in 1964 that he had handed a copy of the first Protocols to Kasztner during the latter's visit to Bratislava late in April 1944;

— The claim of Neumann that these Protocols were sent to Hungary, Switzerland and the Vatican "shortly" after they had been completed;

— Vrba's claim that he was assured by Neumann and Krasznyansky on April 26 that the reports were already in the hands of Kasztner;

— The assertion by Munkácsi that the Protocols were handled in Hungary in a "confidential" manner in order "not to create panic" among the remaining Jews;

— The claim that Kasztner deliberately remained silent in accordance with an agreement with Eichmann under which he was allowed to save a few thousand "prominent" Jews, including his own family and friends.

It is safe to *presume* that Krasznyansky's contention about Kasztner's visit to Bratislava is correct. It is also safe to accept Krasznyansky's claim to have translated the first Protocols into Hungarian and forwarded them to Hungary "within two weeks," i.e., around May 10. Krasznyansky, after all, played a pivotal role in the preparation and distribution of the Protocols. Moreover, Kasztner was a frequent visitor in Bratislava, especially after he had established contact with the SS early in April. He must obviously have been eager to consult the leaders of the Bratislava Rescue Committee, who had considerable experience in dealing with Wisliceny and other members of the Eichmann *Sonderkommando.*

Accordingly, given the evidence that by the time of the German occupation of Hungary both Kasztner and the official leaders of Hungarian Jewry were aware of the Nazis' extermination program, how can one explain their silence? To take Kasztner first: a case against him (and indirectly against some of his closest associates in the provinces and in Budapest) was made after the war by both Jews and non-Jews using a variety of political-ideological, historical-moral, and judicial arguments.

In his postwar "memoirs" Eichmann, for example, argued that he and Kasztner, the two "idealists" who pursued different and conflicting objectives, reached a "gentlemen's agreement" whereby Kasztner allegedly offered to remain silent (and "help keep the Jews from resisting deportation and even keep order in the collection camps") for the opportunity to rescue 15,000 to 20,000 "biologically valuable" Jews. For Eichmann this was a good bargain, since he could disregard the escape of small groups of Jews.[76] His primary concern was the orderly deportation of nearly 800,000 Hungarian Jews without encountering another "Warsaw uprising."

The same conclusion was reached by a number of anti-Zionist or anti-Mapai Zionist figures, including Vrba and Ben Hecht. According to them, Kasztner and his friends (both in Hungary and elsewhere) constituted a group of quislings that sold out Hungarian Jewry to save themselves, their friends, and a few rich Jews. A somewhat similar line has been taken by Communist historians and propagandists. The anti-Jewish drive in the Soviet bloc, launched in September 1948 and presented as a campaign against "Zionism and cosmopolitanism," has sought to identify Zionism with Nazism. As part of this still continuing campaign, Kasztner's activities have been portrayed as an example of Zionism and Nazism finding a common interest in the destruction of vast numbers of innocent people.[77]

At the judicial level, by far the most damning conclusion concerning Kasztner was reached by Judge Benjamin Halevi at the original Grünwald Trial. In his verdict, Halevi asserted that Kasztner and his colleagues in Kolozsvár and Nagyvárad, whom the Jewish masses had trusted, allowed themselves to be used by the SS in their calculated plan to mislead the Jews by spreading the false information about Kenyérmezö. They did everything in their power to soothe the Jews in the ghettos and prevent resistance; in return the Nazis allowed Kasztner to rescue close to 2,000 "prominent Jews."[78] A similar conclusion was reached by Judge Moshe Silberg of the Supreme Court of Israel in his minority opinion against the reversal of Judge Halevi's verdict.

As for the silence of the leaders of the Budapest Jewish Council, the interpretations offered after the war naturally also vary. Ilona Benoschofsky,[79] for example, argues that they perhaps thought that "since Hungarian Jewry cannot be saved, it is better that it does not know the fate awaiting it. And since the Germans threatened to execute those who speak of deportation, the Council did not assist in publicizing the real objective of the deportation, namely the gas chamber and the crematorium."[80] She adds that if "the Jewish Council thought that there was no way out for the masses, there was one for itself."[81]

Ironically, a related argument was advanced by Chaim Cohen, the then Attorney General of Israel, in defending Kasztner against the accusation of collaboration with the SS. He claimed that Kasztner, convinced that there was no hope for the Jews of Hungary, did not disclose the secret of the extermination in order not to frustrate the rescue of the few.[82] Judge Shlomo Chesin of the Supreme Court agreed with this line of reasoning, arguing that Kasztner "didn't warn Hungarian Jewry of the danger facing it because he didn't think it would be useful, and because he thought that any deeds resulting from information given them would damage more than help...."[83]

According to the arguments just mentioned, Kasztner followed in the footsteps of Rabbi Dr. Leo Baeck, the former Chairman of the

Reich Association of the Jews in Germany. While in Theresienstadt, where he had been deported from Berlin on January 27, 1943, Baeck was fully aware of the realities of the Nazi's extermination program. Nevertheless, as he later explained:

> I finally decided that no one should know it. If the Council of Elders were informed, the whole camp would know within a few hours. Living in the expectation of death by gassing would only be the harder and this death was not certain at all: there was selection for slave labor, perhaps not all transports went to Auschwitz. So I came to the grave decision to tell no one.[84]

So much for some of the arguments for and against. All of them are beside the point in one respect. As indicated earlier they do not explain or justify the silence of Jewish leaders *before* the German occupation. However relevant they may be to the desperate situation of Hungarian Jewry *after* the occupations of March 1944, they are irrelevant to the earlier period.

Perhaps the biggest mistakes were made when Hungarian Jews were still relatively well off, when precautionary measures might have minimized the catastrophe, if not totally averted it. Although the official Hungarian Jewish leadership and the leading Zionists were remarkably aware of Nazi anti-Jewish actions elsewhere, they failed to inform the masses authoritatively and to heed the advice of Polish and Slovak refugees to take precautionary measures. As good law-abiding citizens, the official Jewish leaders heeded the censorship regulations and avoided using their organs for such "propaganda" purposes. The sermons in the synagogues at best only alluded to the suffering of the Jews in Nazi-occupied countries in rather general terms.

As a result the Hungarian Jews, living so close to Auschwitz, had no sure knowledge about the gas chambers, or about the mass murders committed further afield by the *SS-Einsatzgruppen*. They discounted what they heard about these horrors as rumors or anti-Nazi propaganda. It was thus even easier for the masses than for their leaders to delude themselves about their relative safety. They rationalized their predicament by arguing that whatever was really happening to the Jews of Poland and elsewhere, such horrors could not possibly take place in Hungary, where the destiny of Jews and Christians had been intertwined for over a thousand years.

The sudden German occupation of Hungary found the Jews not only uninformed about the Nazis' Final Solution program, but also generally disunited. Little effort had been made to end the constant bickering within and between the three major official (Neolog, Orthodox, and Status Quo) communities and the semi-illegal Zionist organization. There were also conflicts between the assimilated-acculturated groups and the Zionists, between the rich and the poor, and between the larger and the semi-autonomous congregations. All this was compounded by the petty jealousy and personal animosity with which many leaders of these communities pursued parochial objectives.

Uninformed, unprepared, and disunited, the Jews were an easy prey for the SS and their Hungarian hirelings. They were isolated and demoralized at lightning speed. The SS acquired exclusive jurisdiction over the Jews during the early and crucial phase of the occupation.[85] The quisling Sztójay government eagerly embraced the anti-Jewish measures suggested by László Baky and László Endre, the two ultra-rightist Secretaries of State who colluded with the SS in planning and implementing the Final Solution in Hungary. The one stratum of Hungarian Christian society on which the official Jewish leaders depended for protection—the aristocratic and conservative leadership with which they had good contacts—was itself decimated in the early phase of the occupation.

Trapped and abandoned by their own government, both the traditional official Jewish leaders and the Zionist ones tried desperately to save what could still be saved under the given conditions. The former tried to win "a race with time" by relying on dilatory tactics and the rapid advance of the Red Army. They consequently continued to employ traditional legal methods, including the filing of appeals and petitions, which had proved highly effective during the preoccupation semi-parliamentary era, but were totally inadequate under Nazi rule. The Zionists, while agreeing with the objectives, if not the tactics, of the traditional Jewish leaders, basically believed that only by direct dealing with the SS, the *real* holders of power in Hungary, could the maximum be achieved for Hungarian Jewry.

In retrospect, both approaches proved equally disastrous.[86] Defying reason and logic, the German and Hungarian Nazis, driven by ideological considerations and a venomous racial hatred, largely succeeded in achieving their objective. This was due not so much to the lack of Jewish resistance,[87] as to the wholehearted support from the Hungarian government and its instruments of power—the civil service, gendarmerie, and police—for implementing the Final Solution program. The success was also assisted by the absence of any meaningful resistance on the part of leftist and democratic forces and by the general passivity of the Christian population.

While the silence of the Hungarian Jewish leaders, like that of the rest of the world, very likely exacerbated the tragedy of Hungarian Jewry, one must bear in mind that responsibility lies first and foremost with the Germans. Dedicated as the Hungarian Nazis were to solving the Jewish question, and poisoned as the Hungarians were by decades of anti-Jewish propaganda, Hungarian Jewry would probably have survived the war relatively intact had the Germans not occupied the country.

NOTES

1. Kasztner, as deputy chairman of the Hungarian Zionist Organization, was involved with Joel Brand in attempting to rescue Hungarian Jews through negotiations with the Germans (and especially Adolf Eichmann). He settled in Israel after the war. There he was accused in 1953 by Malkiel Grünwald of complicity in the destruction of Hungarian Jewry. A libel suit against Grünwald was decided in the latter's favor by a lower court in 1955 after a brilliant defense by his counsel Shmuel Tamir. In 1958 the Israeli Supreme Court reversed the decision—a year after Kasztner had been murdered in the street following the controversy surrounding the earlier trial.

2. Ernö Munkácsi, the executive secretary of the Jewish community of Pest, asserted that the Hungarian Jewish leaders were then "more or less aware of the fate of German Jewry and of the fact that the Jewish population in the Nazi-occupied countries were deported." However, he continued, only "indefinite and nebulous news were spread about all these things." Ernö Munkácsi, *Hogyan történt?* ("How Did It Happen?"; Budapest, 1947), p. 11.

3. On the Wannsee Conference, see Raul Hilberg, *The Destruction of the European Jews* (Chicago, 1961), pp. 264-66. On "Killing Center Operations" see pp. 555-635; on *Einsatzgruppen*, see pp. 242-56.

4. Randolph L. Braham, "The Kamenets Podolsk and Délvidék Massacres: Prelude to the Holocaust in Hungary," *Yad Vashem Studies*, 9 (1973), 133-56.

5. Arthur D. Morse, *While Six Million Died* (New York, 1968), pp. 304-5. Kasztner admitted that the tragedy of the Jews in Nazi-occupied Eastern Europe could be followed clearly from Budapest and that by late Summer 1941 he and his colleagues had solid information about the mass executions in the Ukraine, the Baltic States, Bessarabia and Bukovina. Around the same time they were also informed through Hungarian agents about the use of gassing vans. See Ernest Landau, ed., *Der Kastner-Bericht* (Munich, 1961), p. 37.

6. Randolph L. Braham, "The Kamenets Podolsk and Délvidék Massacres," *op. cit.*, p. 142.

7. Henry L Feingold, *The Politics of Rescue: The Roosevelt Administration and the Holocaust 1938-1945* (New Brunswick, N.J., 1970), p. 168.

8. Livia Rothkirchen, *Hurban yahadut Slovakia* (intn. in English; Jerusalem, 1961), pp. xxiii-xxiv (on the escapes from the first transports), xxxii; *Der Kastner-Bericht, op. cit.*, pp. 15-16. That the Vatican informed Tuka about the killing of the "resettled" Slovak Jews was also confirmed by Hans Gmelin, the former Counselor to the German Legation in Bratislava (NO-5921).

9. Yehuda Bauer, "When Did They Know?", *Midstream*, Apr. 1968, pp. 51-58 (contains the text of the Bund report in Polish original and English translation).

10. For details on Sommer's background and revelations, see Edgar Salin, "Über Artur Sommer, den Menschen und List-Forscher," *Mitteilungen der List Gesellschaft* (Basel), Nov. 30, 1967, pp. 81-90 (quotation from pp. 85-86).

11. Riegner stated that Sagalowitz was also his source in a letter to the editors of *Das Neue Israel* (Zurich) on Arthur D. Morse's *While Six Million Died, op. cit.* (note 5 above). See *Das Neue Israel*, Nov. 1968, pp. 359-61. The role of Pozner is reviewed by Shlomo Derech in his introduction to the Hebrew version of Morse's work, *Ve-ha-olam shatak et nispu shishah milyonim* (Tel Aviv, 1972). Note that the way in which the British are said to have first received the information is also different than in Morse's account.

12. The Budapest Rescue Committee operated as a branch of the United Rescue Committee of the Jewish Agency in Jerusalem. For a critical review of its activities, see Aryeh Morgenstern, "Vaad ha-hatzala ha-me'uhad she-le-yad ha-Sokhnut ha-Yehudit u-fe'ulotav," *Yalkut Moreshet*, 13 (June 1971), pp. 60-103.

13. Alex Weissberg, *Advocate for the Dead: The Story of Joel Brand* (London, 1958), pp. 30-31. Kasztner reported that one of the primary functions of the Rescue Committee was to transmit abroad "reports about the mass murders in the East"; see *Der Kastner-Bericht, op. cit.*, p. 26. In a taped interview with this writer on October 10, 1972, Hansi Brand, who also played an important role in the Rescue Committee, asserted that the Committee had received information about gassings in Poland in 1942 and that Hermann Adler had informed it in 1943 about the building of crematoria. All this information, she claimed, was forwarded to the Jewish Agency unit in Istanbul.

14. On her see the WIZO booklet by Y.O. Neumann, *Gisi Fleischmann: The Story of a Heroic Woman* (Tel Aviv, 1970).

15. Kasztner acknowledged that Gisi Fleischmann transmitted authenticated personal accounts about "the mass executions and gassings abroad". See *Der Kastner-Bericht, op. cit.*, p. 28, and also Livia Rothkirchen, *Hurban yahadut Slovakia, op. cit.*, p. xxviii.

16. It was Rabbi Weissmandel who had obtained information about the railways agreement and who had also sent a copy of the so-called Auschwitz Protocols (on which

more below) to Fülöp (Philipp de) Freudiger. See Weissmandel's *Min ha-metzar* (New York, 1960) and also Livia Rothkirchen, *Hurban yahadut Slovakia, op. cit.*, pp. xxvi and xli.

17. *Der Kastner-Bericht, op. cit.*, p. 82.

18. On the "Europa Plan," see Livia Rothkirchen, *Hurban yahadut Slovakia, op. cit.*, and also Yad Vashem file M-20/93. Wisliceny had "established his credentials" with the Jewish leaders by his role in halting the Slovakian deportations in Fall 1942.

19. Yad Vashem File M-20/93 (which contains most of her reports and letters, written in German).

20. *Ibid.*

21. *Ibid.*

22. See, for example, the reports dated "Budapest, Aug. 23, 1943" and "Sept. 1943" at Beit Lohamei Hagetaot, the Yitzhak Katsenelson Institute in Israel, under file nos. G1054/5, G1054/8, and G1054/3.

23. The above information was supplied in personal communications to this author from Teicholz on June 28, 1971 and from Adler on February 10, 1975. On Anton Schmidt, the German army sergeant who cooperated with the Jewish underground in Vilna and Bialystok (providing its members especially with false documentation and transport facilities), until caught and executed by the Gestapo, see Gideon Hausner, *Justice in Jerusalem* (New York, 1966), p. 258.

24. Samu Stern, "A Race with Time," in Randolph L. Braham, ed., *Hungarian-Jewish Studies*, vol. 3 (New York, 1973), pp. 5-6. Italics added.

25. *Der Kastner-Bericht* is a published version of this report.

26. *Der Kastner-Bericht, op. cit.*, pp. 21, 26, 77 and *passim.*

27. *Ministries Case*, Court 4, Case 11, session of March 19, 1948, transcript p. 3622.

28. *Ibid.*, pp. 3651-3652.

29. See note 1 above.

30. Ben Hecht, *Perfidy* (New York, 1961), pp. 59-60. Hecht's version of Kasztner's testimony (and of the trial) is highly condensed. For Kasztner's complete testimony (in Hebrew) of Feb. 18, 1954, see District Court, Jerusalem, *Criminal Case 124/53*, at the YIVO Institute for Jewish Research, New York, Film 221 M, Roll 2, p. 9.

31. In his judgment acquitting Grünwald, Judge Halevi recalled Danzig's testimony that he had first learned about the realities of Auschwitz after he got to the "Columbus Camp" in Budapest, where the so-called Kasztner group was housed before its departure for Bergen Belsen on June 30, 1944. See *Psak din shel beit ha-mishpat ha-mehozi...neged Malkiel Grünwald...* (Tel Aviv, 1957), p. 16. Hecht's description of Danzig's testimony in *Perfidy, op. cit.*, p. 108, is over-condensed.

32. In the interview Hermann, who was secretary of the Kolozsvár Jewish Council, claimed that he did not meet with Kasztner during the latter's visit in May 1944 and did not know who had met him. Hermann denied any knowledge of the extermination, except the "horror stories" he had heard from the Polish and Slovak refugees; he was convinced, like most Jews, that the deportees were being taken for labor.

33. In her taped interview Hansi Brand stated that it was "inconceivable that [these individuals] did not know what the German occupation meant in March-April 1944." She further insisted that the leaders of Kolozsvár had been informed exactly about what was happening to the Jews in Poland even *before* Kasztner's visit in May 1944.

34. Kenyérmezö was basically a fictitious geographic name like "Waldsee." During World War I, there was a military training camp near Esztergom that bore the name of Kenyérmezö. The rumors about Kenyérmezö and Transdanubia were also spread by the gendarmes just before the deportation.

35. Ben Hecht, *Perfidy*, *op. cit.*, pp. 105-8.

36. For details see *Der Kastner-Bericht*, *op. cit.*

37. Compare Bela Vago, "Political and Diplomatic Activities for the Rescue of the Jews of Northern Transylvania," *Yad Vashem Studies*, 6 (1967), 155-73.

38. Ben Hecht, *Perfidy*, *op. cit.*, pp. 117-18.

39. According to Erich Kulka, 280 attempts at escape were noted during the existence of Auschwitz and about 80 prisoners actually succeeded in escaping. Erich Kulka, "Five Escapes from Auschwitz," in Yuri Suhl, ed., *They Fought Back* (New York, 1967), p. 201.

40. *Ibid.*, pp. 196-205.

41. Rosenberg acquired false identification papers bearing the name of Rudolf Vrba, a name which he has kept permanently. His own account appears in his *I Cannot Forgive* (New York, 1964), written in cooperation with Alan Bestic.

42. Wetzler, who was given the name Josef Lanik, published under the latter name *Oswiecim, hrobka styroch milionov ludi* (Auschwitz, Tomb of Four Million People; 2nd ed., Kosice, 1946) and *Co Dante nevidil* (What Dante Did Not See; Bratislava, 1964).

43. Statement by Krasznyansky, Institute of Contemporary Jewry (Hebrew University), Oral History Division, Catalog no. 3, 1970, p. 120, no. 410 S.E. Protocol in Czech, pp. 10 and 13.

44. The Auschwitz Protocols may be found, *inter alia*, at the Yad Vashem Institute Archives in Jerusalem under no. M-20/149. For their Hungarian version see Munkácsi, *Hogyan történt?*, *op. cit.*, note 2 above, pp. 88-110.

45. Erich Kulka, "Five Escapes from Auschwitz," *op. cit.*, pp. 206-7.

46. Burzio, the Papal Nuncio, was expected to deliver it to the Vatican and Kasztner was expected to hand over copies to Admiral Horthy and the Prince Primate, Jusztinián Cardinal Serédi. The Protocols were translated into Yiddish by Rabbi Weissmandel.

47. For other details see Erich Kulka, "Five Escapes from Auschwitz," *op. cit.*, pp. 207-11.

48. Rudolf Vrba and Alan Bestic, *I Cannot Forgive*, *op. cit.*, p. 250.

49. Oscar Neumann, *Im Schatten des Todes* (Tel Aviv, 1956), pp. 178-82.

50. Personal communication to this author on Nov. 19, 1972.

51. Personal communication to this author on February 7, 1973. In his interview in Jerusalem in 1964, Krasznyansky stated that "a copy of the Protocols was handed over to Dr. Kasztner." Institute of Contemporary Jewry, Oral History Division, catalog no. 3, 1970, p. 117, no. 398. Protocol in German, pp. 5-6.

52. *Hungarian-Jewish Studies*, vol. 3, *op. cit.*, note 24 above, p. 14.

53. *Ibid.*, pp. 52 and 56.

54. *Ibid.*, pp. 74-142. In his epilogue of November 21, 1972 (pp. 143-46), however, Freudiger claims that "by the time [they] learned the truth about Auschwitz, the first phase of the deportation, involving some 310,000 Jews, was already over." That phase, involving the Jews of Carpatho-Ruthenia and Transylvania, came to an end on June 7, 1944.

55. The circumstances under which he received a copy of the Protocols are described in his *Five Months* (manuscript dated November 21, 1972), p. 19.

56. Erich Kulka, "Auschwitz Condoned," *The Wiener Library Bulletin*, vol. 23, no. 1, New Series, no. 14 (Winter 1968), p. 3.

57. Munkácsi, *Hogyan történt?*, *op. cit.*, p. 111.

58. Taped interview with Fábián Herskovits (Oct. 9, 1972), and personal communication by Lea Fürst (Oct. 13, 1972). The Pope in fact knew German.

59. Manoliu, who had good, and apparently lucrative, relations with Mantello, got in touch with Krausz in Budapest at the request of Mantello. The latter, in turn, was contacted for this purpose by Dr. Chaim Pozner, who as head of the Palestine Office of Geneva was Krausz's counterpart in Switzerland, and whose note Manoliu took along to Budapest as his "letter of accreditation." For the text of Krausz's letter and reports, see Yad Vashem Archives, M-20/95.

60. *Ibid.*, M-20/47.

61. Secret World War II documents published by the Vatican on April 4, 1973, prove that aides to Pope Pius XII (including the future Popes John XXIII and Paul VI), and presumably the Pope himself, already knew of the Nazi slaughter of Jews. See Paul Hofmann, "The Vatican Knew of Nazi Pogroms, Its Records Show," *New York Times*, April 5, 1973, and "Pius Knew in 1941 of Drive on Jews," *ibid.*, April 27, 1974. See further Saul Friedländer, *Pius XII and the Third Reich* (New York, 1966), esp. pp. 103 ff. and 236-38; also Carlo Falconi, *The Silence of Pius XII* (Boston, 1970).

62. Vrba allots only a few paragraphs to the Sväty Jur meeting and completely ignores the presence and role of Mordowicz: *I Cannot Forgive*, *op. cit.*, pp. 256-57. For Krasznyansky's version of the meeting see Erich Kulka, "Five Escapes from Auschwitz," *op. cit.*, p. 210.

63. For the text of the Pope's note and Horthy's reply of July 1, 1944, see Lévai, *Szürke könyv magyar zsidok megmentéséröl* (Grey Book on the Rescuing of Hungarian Jews; Budapest, 1946), p. 21.

64. *Ibid.*, pp. 56-57.

65. For the text of King Gustav V's telegram of June 30 and Horthy's reply of July 1, see *ibid.*, pp. 72-73.

66. In a letter to Vrba dated May 18, 1964, Mantello made the following comments on the reports he had received from Budapest: "These reports...were short and arrived in Switzerland rather late.... If we had received your complete report about six or seven weeks earlier, say about the same time that you had sent it to Budapest, perhaps we could have put a stop to the deportations, since we would have started a big press campaign in Switzerland and abroad." Erich Kulka, "Five Escapes from Auschwitz," *op. cit.*, pp. 217-18.

67. A brief, unofficial reference to the Protocols and their contents appeared in the *New York Times* ("Inquiry Confirms Nazi Death Camps") of July 3, 1944. Judging by Raphael Vago's research, the Protocols were also unnoticed or ignored by the Palestine press, including the Hebrew language press. See his "The Destruction of Hungarian Jewry as Reflected in the Palestine Press," *Hungarian-Jewish Studies*, vol. 3, *op. cit.*, pp. 291-324. This although the Jewish Telegraphic Agency (under the dateline London, July 10, 1944) issued an account based on the Protocols, which were most probably supplied by Mantello.

68. Horthy wrongly claims that the secret information about the extermination camps reached him only in August. Admiral Nicholas Horthy, *Memoirs* (New York, 1957), p. 219.

69. Randolph L. Braham, *The Destruction of Hungarian Jewry* (New York, 1963), vol. I, pp. 218ff.

70. M. Szinai and L. Szücs, eds., *The Confidential Papers of Admiral Horthy* (Budapest, 1965), pp. 248-57.

71. Randolph L. Braham, "The Holocaust in Hungary: An Historical Interpretation of the Role of the Hungarian Radical Right," *Societas*, vol. 2, no. 3 (Summer 1972), p. 202.

72. *Der Kastner-Bericht, op. cit.*, p. 302.

73. Israel Police, Bureau 06, doc. no. 1319.

74. *Der Kastner-Bericht, op. cit.*, p. 49.

75. Ilona Benoschofsky and Elek Karsai, eds., *Vádirat a nácizmus ellen* (Indictment of Nazism; Budapest, 1958), vol. 1, p. 317.

76. "Eichmann Tells His Own Damning Story," *Life*, Dec. 5, 1960, p. 146.

77. For samples on this theme from a variety of Communist newspapers, consult *Jews in Eastern Europe*, a periodical newsletter edited by Emanuel Litvinoff and issued by European Jewish Publications of London.

78. See *Psak din shel beit ha-mishpat ha-mehozi..., op. cit.*, pp. 22-24 ff. and 45. Also Ben Hecht, *Perfidy, op. cit.*, pp. 178-83.

79. Miss Benoschofsky is known as the Director of the Jewish Museum of Budapest, as well as being a co-editor of the first two volumes of *Vádirat a nácizmus ellen* cited above (note 75).

80. *Vádirat a nácizmus ellen, op. cit.*, vol. 2, p. 44.

81. In justification of this remark (*ibid.*, pp. 44-45), she argues that since the anti-Jewish measures of the Horthy era, including the major anti-Jewish laws, affected primarily the little Jews (the lower civil servants, small traders and artisans), the members of the Jewish Council, "who knew of these restrictive measures largely only by hearsay, obviously had hoped that they would be exempted this time as well."

82. As quoted by Judge Moshe Silberg in Ben Hecht, *Perfidy, op. cit.*, p. 273. For the Hebrew original see *Arar Plili 232/55, berur shel ha-me'ar'er: Ha-yo'etz ha-mishpati la-memshala neged Malkiel Grunwald* (duplicated by the Students' Union of the Hebrew University, Jerusalem, 1957).

83. Ben Hecht, *Perfidy, op. cit.*, p. 270; *Arar Plili 232/55 op. cit.*, pp. 174-97.

84. Eric H. Boehm, ed., *We Survived—The Stories of Fourteen of the Hidden and the Hunted of Nazi Germany* (New Haven, 1949), p. 293. The matter is discussed further in Jacob Robinson's introduction to Isaiah Trunk, *Judenrat* (New York, 1972).

85. *Inter alia*, through the Hitler-Horthy agreement of March 18, 1944; see my "The Holocaust in Hungary," *op. cit.*, note 71 above.

86. The leaders of the Jewish Council claim that their tactics saved the Jews of Budapest. The Zionists claim credit for having saved close to an additional 20,000 Jews—some 1,700 in the so-called Kasztner group and around 18,000 in Strasshof, Austria.

87. By the time the Jews were placed in the ghettos, they had been deprived of their dignity and property. It is likely that even if they had been told the truth they could not have organized any meaningful resistance in the absence of many of the able-bodied males in the labor companies. Moreover, the Jews were not psychologically prepared to accept the truth by that time.

3

The Hungarian Press, 1938-1945

The Holocaust clearly demonstrated the validity of the maxim that the pen is at least as mighty, if not mightier, than the sword. The power of the word was exploited by the Nazis and their accomplices all over Europe, as evidenced by the emphasis they placed on propaganda. The Nazis' propaganda campaign aimed to create a climate of opinion that would make their diabolical plans for the "solution of the Jewish question" acceptable. This was clearly reflected in the prosecution statement in the Nuremberg trial of Julius Streicher, the publisher of the rabidly anti-Semitic *Der Stürmer*:

> No government in the world, before the Nazis came to power, could have embarked upon and put into effect a policy of mass extermination without having a people who would back them and support them. It was to the task of educating people, of producing murderers, educating and poisoning them with hate that Streicher set himself.... He made these crimes possible which could never have happened had it not been for him and for those like him....[1]

Like other countries in Nazi-dominated Europe, Hungary too was cursed with many journalists and xenophobic intellectuals agitating in Streicher's vein. These were associated with ultra-Rightist political movements and parties that had at their disposal large number of anti-Semitic press organs. Collectively, they fostered a climate of opinion that conditioned the Hungarian public to acquiesce in the increasingly severe anti-Jewish policies of the various governments, including those enacted during the Holocaust.

Although the tone of the anti-Jewish drive became particularly abrasive following the adoption of the first major anti-Jewish law in 1938, the climate of intolerance was created after the end of World

---

Scheduled for publication in *Journalism and the Holocaust*, Robert Moses Shapiro, ed. (New York: Yeshiva University Press, 1999). Printed with permission of the editor.

War I. The disintegration of the Austro-Hungarian Empire and the truncating of Hungary not only put an end to the relatively short-lived "Golden Era" of Hungarian Jewry,[2] but eventually also brought to power a fundamentally anti-Semitic counterrevolutionary regime that ruled the country until the end of World War II. This regime was supported primarily by disgruntled officers who had lost their positions, the fixed-income middle and lower middle classes that were severely hit by the ever steeper inflationary spiral, and the large number of public servants and property owners who escaped from or were expelled by the authorities of the Successor States.[3] These disgruntled elements were susceptible to being swayed by demagogue-intellectuals placing the blame for their suffering on the "alien" Jews. As the authors and embodiments of an ideology which came to be known as the "Szeged Idea" (*A szegedi gondolat*)—a nebulous amalgam of political propagandistic views incorporating the concepts of anti-Bolshevism, anti-Semitism, chauvinistic nationalism, and revisionism—these Rightist intellectuals were in fact the forerunners of Hungarian proto-Fascism. Many among them were journalists and editors associated with a variety of anti-Semitic press organs.

The real strongholds of power supporting the champions of the Szeged Idea were the many secret and semi-clandestine patriotic associations and paramilitary organizations that were not only tolerated but actively encouraged and secretly supported by the counterrevolutionary governments. Using their groups' press organs, the leaders of these associations and organizations arrogated to themselves the power and responsibility to defend "the Magyar cause" by spreading the virulent seeds of revisionism, irredentism, anti-liberalism, and, above all, anti-Semitism. They depicted Jews as "aliens" hostile to the Christian body politic and inimical to the national interests of Hungary. Through the press organs to which they had access, they helped propagate the Nazi myth about the Jews by depicting them as being at once exploiters and revolutionaries, both plutocrats and Bolsheviks. After the collapse of the multinational Hungarian kingdom, the Jews emerged as the most vulnerable minority group. In contrast to the so-called Golden Era when the Jewish question was politically and officially suppressed, in Trianon Hungary the Jews, having lost their importance as statistical recruits to the cause of Magyardom, found themselves exploited as scapegoats for the country's political and economic disasters.

The anti-Jewish campaign gained considerable momentum in 1932-33 with the almost simultaneous acquisition of power by Gyula Gömbös in Hungary and Hitler in Germany. The foremost representative and leader of the Hungarian Radical Right, Gömbös managed during his four-year tenure as prime minister (1932-1936) to tie Hungary's destiny almost irrevocably to Nazi Germany's. He brought Hungary's foreign policy into line with that of the Third Reich and made possible the subsequent penetration and direct involvement of the National Socialists in practically every aspect of the country's life. By replacing large segments of the civil and military bureaucracies of the state apparatus with his own proteges and packing the upper army hierarchy, including the General Staff, with younger, highly nationalistic Germanophile officers, Gömbös brought about the establishment of a collaborationist power base in Hungary which later proved fatal to Hungarian Jewry.

Perhaps the most successful achievement of the Nazis during the Gömbös period was the radicalization of the press. The Third Reich was quite generous in supporting the publication of a large number of vitriolically anti-Semitic dailies and weeklies like *Új Magyarság* (New Magyardom), *Magyarság* (Magyardom), *Virradat* (Dawn), *Magyar Futár* (Hungarian Courier), *Nemzetör* (National Guard), *Összetartás* (Unity), and *Pesti Újság* (Journal of Pest). The journalists and editors of these publications spewed an incessantly pro-Nazi and virulently anti-Semitic propaganda barrage that poisoned Hungarian public opinion and prepared the ground for the general acceptance of the increasingly severe measures adopted against the Jews.[4] Toward the end of the 1930s, the Jewish question became a major national obsession, frequently rivaling revisionism in the intensity of feeling it aroused. Emulating its Nazi counterpart, the Hungarian radical press became ever more shrill in depicting the Jews as naturally unpatriotic, parasites sapping the energy of the nation, and agents of both Soviet communism and Western capitalism. The propaganda campaign was soon coupled with demands for a definitive solution of the Jewish question. The suggestions offered by the radicals ranged from legal restrictions on the Jews' professional and economic activities to their orderly "resettlement" out of the country.

The anti-Semitic press also played a leading role in crystallizing the ideas and championing the cause of the various Right-radical movements and parties that challenged the legitimacy of the ruling elites on whom the Jews depended for their survival.[5] Having embraced the Third Reich for its opposition to Bolshevism and support for Hungarian revisionism, Hungary's conservative-aristocratic governments were soon compelled to come to grips with the ever more influential Right radicals at home. While they despised and feared these radicals even more than they did the Jews—the Hungarian ultra-Rightists had advocated not only solving the Jewish question, but also bringing about a social revolution to end the inherited privileges of the ruling elites—the governmental leaders felt compelled to appease them. In fact, they soon looked upon the Right radicals' preoccupation with the Jewish question as a blessing in disguise, for it helped deflect attention from the grave social-agrarian problems confronting the nation.

While opposing the domestic political and socioeconomic agenda of the Right radicals, the ruling aristocratic-conservative forces shared some of the ideas advanced by them. These included the issue of territorial revisionism, the pursuit of national-Christian, anti-Bolshevik policies, and the need to urgently "solve" the Jewish question. But while the ruling elite adopted a relatively moderate Italian-type semi-Fascist position, the Right radicals were eager to embrace the German brand of National Socialism. This division in the political Right was reflected especially in the approach to the "solution" of the Jewish question. The aristocratic-conservative-dominated ruling wing, which had good connections with the Jewish upper class, attempted to implement a "civilized" anti-Semitic program calculated not only to gradually diminish and eventually eliminate the Jews' influence from the country's economic and cultural life, but also to appease the Right radicals at home and the National Socialists abroad. While recognizing the danger of German expansionism, this group felt a need to keep on good terms with the Third Reich, primarily for the advancement of Hungary's revisionist objectives. The Right radical wing, on the other hand, was politically and ideologically attracted and firmly committed to Nazism. It wholeheartedly embraced the National Socialist program not only because of its anti-Semitism, though this was its most attractive aspect, but also because of its emphasis on social and political reforms that agreed with their own platform.

Whatever the differences in domestic and foreign policy objectives and tactics, a common denominator in the ideologies of these two wings of the political Right was their preoccupation with the "solution" of the Jewish question. The official press organs of the ruling Hungarian Life Party (*Magyar Élet Pártja*—MÉP)—including *Függetlenség* (Independence) and *Esti Újság* (Evening Journal)—and those of the Government—*Pester Lloyd* and *Magyarország* (Hungary)—were often as nauseating on this issue as the openly Nazi papers. This stance reflected primarily the position of the Right wing of the ruling elite, which the "moderates" often also felt compelled to adopt for reasons of political expediency.

Despite the exacerbating anti-Jewish climate and the close cooperation with the Third Reich, which enabled Hungary to fulfill some of its revisionist ambitions,[6] the aristocratic-conservative government permitted the publication of several opposition papers. The most important among these were *Népszava* (People's Voice), organ of the Social Democratic Party, the independent *Magyar Nemzet* (Hungarian Nation), *Mai Nap* (Today), the liberal *Pesti Napló* (Journal of Pest), *Újság* (Journal), *8 Órai Újság* (The 8 O'clock Journal), and *Esti Kurir* (Evening Courier), which often provided objective and balanced accounts of the major issues confronting the country.

A fateful turn for the worse came early in 1938, when Hungary adopted the first major anti-Jewish law. Among other things, the law restricted the proportion of Jews employed in the free professions, including journalism, to 20 percent. Under the second major anti-Jewish law, which was adopted a year later, the proportion was reduced to six percent. Both laws were adopted with the wholehearted support of the Christian Church leaders. The reaction of the press to these anti-Jewish measures was predictable: the Rightist press supported them enthusiastically, hailing the beginning of the drive designed to end the alleged Jewish domination over the country's cultural and economic life. The opposition press deplored the measures and hinted at the influence of the Third Reich in their adoption. Its tone, like the protest by some of Hungary's leading writers and artists, was considerably less critically assertive with regard to the second anti-Jewish law than with regard to the first, although the second one was much more restrictive. Under the provisions of this second anti-Jewish law, Jews were prohibited, among other things, from holding leading positions in the non-Jewish press. The prohibition affected reporters, editors, responsible editors, and publishers of newspapers and periodicals. Following the adoption of this law, the opposition press generally restricted itself to the publication of the major provisions of the law and of the decrees relating to its enactment, without taking real editorial positions against them.

The press-related anti-Jewish measures were adopted on the initiative of the Press Division (*Sajtóosztály*) in the prime minister's office, which had since the end of 1938 been under the leadership of Mihály Kolosváry-Borcsa.[7] A notorious anti-Semite, Kolosváry-Borcsa was a member of the lower house of the Hungarian Parliament representing Pest-Pilis-Solt-Kiskun County and served as the editor of *Függetlenség*, one of the ruling party's official organs. Under his leadership, the Press Division was used as a vehicle to curtail not only the Jewish journalists but also those associated with the relatively weak liberal and leftist press. It enthusiastically implemented the provisions of Press Law No. XVIII of 1938, under which the licenses of newspaper publishers were subjected to thorough political scrutiny designed to curtail and eventually eliminate the Jews' role in the press. This measure, coupled with the introduction of prior censorship and strict supervision of newsprint utilization, compelled 430 mostly smaller newspapers to end publication by early 1939.[8] In addition, a large number of Jewish journalists and editors lost their positions by being purged from membership in the Press Chamber (*Sajtókamara*). In 1941, only 1,572 of the 3,435 applicants for membership in the Press Chamber were admitted, with hardly any Jews among them.[9] The drive against Jewish journalists was also pursued through the cooperation of the ministry of defense, which drafted many of them into the military forced labor service system. Many of these journalists, including some of the most influential figures of the Hungarian press, were assigned to labor service companies that were deployed in the Ukraine and Serbia. Only a few managed to return home after the war.[10]

The opposition press was generally ineffective in counteracting either the anti-Jewish measures of the government or the anti-Semitic onslaught of the Right radical press. This impotence was also the hallmark of the small and increasingly restricted Jewish press, which followed a generally assimilationist, pro-Magyar, patriotic, anti-Zionist line. One of the first victims of the anti-democratic press policies of the Hungarian authorities was *Egyenlöség* (Equality), the country's largest Jewish weekly. Launched in 1882, the weekly was supported primarily by the non-Orthodox strata of Hungarian Jewry. It ceased publication in December 1938 and was succeeded a month later by *A Magyar Zsidók Lapja* (Journal of Hungarian Jews). The new weekly followed the editorial stance of its predecessor, reflecting the assimilationist patriotic posture of the central leadership of Hungarian Jewry. After the outbreak of World War II, *A Magyar Zsidók Lapja* became, for a while at least, Hungarian Jewry's only newspaper. All the other Hungarian- or Yiddish-language papers were compelled to cease publication. The ban affected the Jewish press in the territories acquired by Hungary both before and after the outbreak of the war as well.[11] In 1940, however, the government permitted the publication of a new Hungarian-language Jewish weekly—*Képes Családi Lapok* (Illustrated Family Journal)—in Budapest. Its title notwithstanding, the weekly was basically non-illustrated and, in accordance with the new regulations, had to identify itself in the subtitle as a "Jewish Journal" (*Zsidó Lap*). This weekly occasionally challenged the policies of the Jewish leaders and devoted more space to issues of emigration and paid more attention to the social and economic problems confronting the Jewish community than *A Magyar Zsidók Lapja*, but it too pursued a basically assimilationist editorial policy. Both weeklies adopted a generally apologetic stance: they tried to evoke the sympathy of the authorities—and indirectly of Christian Hungarians—by featuring articles on the contribution of Hungarian Jews to the enrichment of Hungary's culture and economy and, above all, on their participation in the country's struggle for independence and during World War I.

While the Jewish and non-Jewish opposition press were under duress, the influence of the Right radical press grew by leaps and bounds. On the eve of World War II, the Rightist press organs were bolstered not only by lavish support from the Third Reich, but also by the virtual free rein they received from the government of Pál Teleki (February 1939-April 1941). They became ever more vocal in advancing the twin causes of Nazism and anti-Semitism. In the forefront of this campaign were the major national dailies *Magyarság*, *Új Magyarság*, *Pesti Újság*, and *Virradat*. These were joined during Teleki's first year in office by three equally anti-Semitic weeklies—*Holnap* (Tomorrow), *A Nép* (The People), and *Nemzeti Élet* (National Life). Even more rabid in their pro-Nazism and anti-Semitism were *Összetartás* (Unity), *Egyedül Vagyunk* (We Are Alone), *Ország* (Country), and the pictorial *Magyar Futár* (Hungarian Courier). The publishers, editors, and journalists associated with these press organs, including Ferenc Rajniss (*Magyar Futár*), Olivér Rupprecht (*Magyarság*), György Oláh (*Egyedül Vagyunk*), Ferenc Vajta (*Ország*), Károly Maróthy (*Pesti Újság*), Gábor Bornemisza (*Összetartás* and *Virradat*), and István Milotay (*Új Magyarság*), poured out an incessant pro-Nazi and anti-Semitic propaganda barrage that poisoned Hungarian public opinion. By fanning the flames of the anti-Jewish psychosis, they laid the foundation for the acceptance of the draconic measures being adopted against the Jews. After Germany's attack on Poland on September 1, 1939, and the consequent outbreak of World War II, the editorial position of most newspapers became even more pro-Nazi, the editors-in-chief having been warned by the prime minister to keep German foreign political interests in mind.

After Hungary joined the Axis in attacking the Soviet Union (June 27, 1941), the anti-Jewish propaganda campaign became more vicious than ever before. Coinciding with the adoption of the openly racist third anti-Jewish law,[12] the press campaign identified the Jews with all the ills of the country. They were blamed not only for Hungary's involvement in the war, but also for all the domestic evils associated with it, including the shortages of goods and the flourishing black market. The Jews were portrayed as "traitorous, unscrupulous, and cheating" throughout Hungarian history—"an alien race with diabolical skills" that represented a clear and present danger to Hungarian society. They were depicted as foreign agents beholden to both Soviet Bolshevism and Western "plutocratic capitalism."

The anti-Semitic Rightist press demanded the emulation of the Third Reich in the "solution" of the Jewish question and offered specific plans for the "resettlement" of the Jews. Urged on by the venomous press campaign and the many anti-Jewish measures of the government, public opinion took a sharp swing to the Right.

The anti-Semitic climate was also exacerbated by some Catholic publications, which were both theologically and culturally anti-Jewish. These further promoted the anti-Semitic indoctrination of the faithful by dwelling on the issue of deicide, blaming the Jews as a whole for the killing of Jesus.[13]

Following the outbreak of hostilities in June 1941, the opposition press became even more ineffective in counteracting the propaganda impact of the Right radicals. This was also true of the main Jewish press organs—the *A Magyar Zsidók Lapja* and the *Képes Családi Lapok*. Like the non-Jewish opposition press in general, they too failed to inform, let alone alert, their readers about the tragedy that was befalling the Jewish communities in Nazi-dominated Europe. The occasional news items about Jewish communities abroad gave the general impression that while anti-Semitism in Hitler's Europe was more intense than ever before, the communities themselves were not threatened by extinction. On August 14, 1941, for example, *A Magyar Zsidók Lapja* reported that German Jews in French labor camps were allowed to petition for voluntary transfer to German labor camps "where they wish to work." In one of the extremely rare, if not the only, reference to the Warsaw Ghetto, it was pointed out in this newspaper that "in the midst of the greatest difficulties and deprivations, there are regular cultural performances there."[14] There is no account about mass starvation and death, or the humiliation and tortures to which the Jews of Warsaw and Poland in general were subjected. There is not even a reference to the Warsaw Ghetto Uprising in any issue.

The same misleading impression is conveyed by the one report in *A Magyar Zsidók Lapja* on the Soviet Jewish POW's in German hands. Quoting the *Israelitisches Wochenblatt* (Jewish Weekly) of Zurich, the Hungarian Jewish paper informs its readers that the Germans transferred the POW's to camps in the Third Reich, where, according to a finding by the Red Cross, their situation was not objectionable.[15] The Hungarian Jewish masses could not possibly suspect from this article that many of the Soviet POW's in general and the Jewish POW's in particular were subjected, like the deported Jews in

Auschwitz and other death camps, to murderous "special treatment" (*Sonderbehandlung*) by the Germans. A similarly false impression was fostered about the fate of the German Jews. On March 12, 1942, for example, when there were hardly any Jews left in Germany, *A Magyar Zsidók Lapja* selectively cited a dispatch from Frankfurt-am-Main to the effect that Dr. Josef Wohlgemuth, the former rector of the rabbinical seminary of Berlin, had died in the local Jewish hospital. Without any reference to the plight of the German Jews since Hitler's coming to power early in 1933, it leaves the impression that the Jews still had their hospitals and implicitly other communal institutions as well.

Misinformation about the plight of the Jews in the Nazi-dominated parts of Europe extended to inaccurate reporting about the suffering of Hungarian Jewish labor servicemen in the Ukraine and elsewhere. While practically every issue of *A Magyar Zsidók Lapja* contained appeals to help the labor servicemen with money and clothing, at no time did these appeals include any accounts of the barbarous treatment of the labor servicemen by many of their commanders and guards as well as the SS. No space was ever allotted to depicting the liquidation of the Jewish communities in the parts of the Ukraine in which many thousands of Hungarian soldiers and Jewish labor servicemen were stationed. Neither was there any account of the roundup and deportation in the summer of 1941 of close to 18,000 "alien" Jews to near Kamenets-Podolsk, where they were murdered by the SS. The same code of silence was generally observed in connection with the massacres that took place in the Újvidék area early in 1942.

Képes Családi Lapok, however, occasionally published news about the suffering and difficulties encountered by Jewish labor servicemen, to the chagrin of the authorities. Upon overstepping the boundaries of censorship in 1943, the weekly was suspended by the minister of the interior.[16]

The general silence of the Jewish press about the realities of the Nazi persecutions was matched by that of the non-Jewish opposition newspapers, including *Népszava* and *Magyar Nemzet*, which were as uninformative about the plight of the Jews in Nazi-dominated Europe as *A Magyar Zsidók Lapja*. While both the Jewish and the opposition organs were quite skillful in occasionally informing their readers about the military reverses of the Axis by using a generally understood coded language, they failed to apply the same technique in connection with the plight of European Jewry. As a consequence the Hungarian Jews, lulled into a state of confidence—they deluded themselves by insisting that "what happened in Poland could not possibly happen in chivalrous Hungary"—were caught totally unprepared when Hungary was occupied by the Germans.

In contrast to the Jewish and non-Jewish opposition press organs, which were basically silent about the anti-Jewish drive in Nazi-dominated Europe, the ultra-Rightist press was engaged in a vast disinformation campaign designed to advance the drive for the "solution" of the Jewish question in Hungary. It dwelt extensively on the Nazis' "resettlement" program in Poland and elsewhere in German-occupied Europe. It projected a positive image of the new Jewish "settlements" in the East, claiming that Jews from all over Europe were involved there in "productive" physical work and no longer depended on "blackmarketeering, swindling, and banking" for making a living. The following report by *Magyarság* was typical of the accounts provided by many other central and local newspapers about ghetto life in Poland:

> The houses are the property of the state, but the Jews live in them totally without cost. They live an undisturbed private life and enjoy full self-government. Their food is good and the supply is abundant, receiving the same ration as the Germans deployed in the East; those engaged in heavy labor get extra rations. Each person disposes of the wages received in his own way. The [ghetto dwellers] almost never deal with the German authorities. They have no need for that because everything proceeds just fine... It is understandable that one of the Jews complained only about one injustice to our reporter, namely that the other [Jews] are still at home dealing and wheeling in their old ways, and he would like that all of them without exception be here.

The failure to reveal the realities of the Nazis' "resettlement" program and the positive portrayal of ghetto life in Poland played into the hands of the Right radicals. The "positive" press accounts not only mollified large segments of Christians, especially the moderates who had some qualms about the "rumored ultimate" fate of the Jews, but also lulled many of the potential victims into inaction. The disinformation accounts, which Jews also read, reinforced in many the belief that the extermination rumors were nothing but anti-Nazi propaganda.

The inciting, propagandistic, anti-Jewish tone of the Budapest-based major Rightist press organs also became the hallmark of most local and provincial newspapers during the war. This was the case not only of those published in Trianon Hungary[17] but also of those in the reacquired territories.[18] With the passage of time many of the formerly democratic or moderate local press organs were transformed into mouthpieces of the Right. The liberal journalists associated with them were either silenced or made to adjust to the new political realities.

The anti-Jewish propaganda of the wartime period was matched by that directed against the Allies in general and the Soviet Union in particular. The press organs vilified the leaders of the Grand Alliance as stooges in the service of the Jews' drive for world domination. Using inflammatory rhetoric, they exploited the themes originally expounded in the *Protocols of the Elders of Zion*, emphasizing the conspiratorial power of the Jews in the anti-Axis alliance. Anti-Allied propaganda included the publication of cartoons, pictures, and articles about Anglo-Saxon "atrocity" bombings of non-military targets, including schools, hospitals, and cultural establishments.

The press campaign against the Jews and the Allies became even more vicious after the German occupation of Hungary on March 19, 1944. With the opposition newspapers eliminated, the ultra-Rightist press became an accomplice in the implementation of the Final Solution program.

The tone and content of the press organs were largely determined and supervised by the newly established Office of the Royal Hungarian Government Commissioner of the Press (*A sajtóügyek m. kir. kormánybiztosa*). The leadership of the office was entrusted to Mihály Kolosváry-Borcsa,[19] the then head of the National Hungarian Press Chamber (*Országos Magyar Sajtókamara*). The chamber operated in conjunction with the National Press Council (*Országos Sajtótanács*) and the Press Division (*Sajtóosztály*) in the Prime Minister's Office. The main function of the Press Division and of the affiliated agencies was to:

— Monitor the press and political literature published in Hungary;

— Inform the press about measures taken by the government and, in certain concrete cases, about the position of the government; and

— Provide direction in all matters relating to the press's policies.

In early 1944, the Press Division was divided into two sections: the Section of Press Policy (*Sajtópolitikai Osztály*) assumed most of the responsibilities of the Division; the Press Administration Section (*Sajtóigazgatási Osztály*) was entrusted, among other things, with the administration of legal matters and the preparation of press-related legislation.[20]

Kolosváry-Borcsa's anti-Jewish propaganda campaign was further orchestrated by two agencies: the Hungarian Royal Propaganda Office for National Defense (*Magyar Királyi Nemzetvédelmi Propagandahivatal*) and the Hungarian Institute for the Researching of the Jewish Question (*A Zsidókérdéstkutató Magyar Intézet*)—the former already in existence before the German occupation, the latter established a few months after it.

The Hungarian Royal Propaganda Office for National Defense was established in April 1942 and served in fact as Hungary's Ministry of Propaganda.[21] With several mass media outlets under its direct control and generously supported by the government, it was primarily concerned with molding public opinion along Axis lines. The Propaganda Office's anti-Jewish tone became especially virulent after the German occupation, when it operated with seven departments. Of these, by far the most important were Department I (National Policies, *Nemzetpolitikai Ügyosztály*), which dealt with propaganda and the molding of public opinion, and Department III (Information, *Tájékoztató Ügyosztály*), which monitored public opinion and guided the press organs involved in shaping it.

The Hungarian Institute for the Researching of the Jewish Question was established in April 1944 and formally inaugurated on May 12.[22] Launched with the advice and guidance of *SS-Hauptsturmführer* Ballensiefen, a Nazi expert on anti-Jewish propaganda, the Institute was placed under the leadership of Zoltán Bosnyák, a notorious Hungarian anti-Semite. According to article 3 of its bylaws, the Institute was to "study the Jewish question in Hungary in a systematic and scientific manner, collect and scientifically process the related data, and inform Hungarian public opinion about the Hungarian and general Jewish question." Its major vehicle for the latter purpose was *Harc* (Battle), a vehemently anti-Jewish weekly modeled after the German *Der Stürmer*.

The anti-Jewish tone and content of the Budapest newspapers and periodicals were echoed by those published in the provinces. They applauded the measures the post-occupation quisling government adopted against the Jews. They printed and gleefully commented on the increasingly severe decrees relating to the isolation, expropriation, ghettoization, and concentration of the Jews. Most of the local newspapers became the mouthpiece of the pro-Nazi regime, enthusiastically supporting all anti-Jewish policies. Many of their feature articles focused attention on loopholes in the existing anti-Jewish legislation, often calling for ever harsher restrictions. Virtually all newspapers praised the "positive" impact of the anti-Jewish measures in the country and aimed to reassure their readers about the ultimate fate of the deported Jews. Many of the articles dealt with the healthier lifestyle that was reportedly created for the Jews in the new "settlements in the East." After the Jews were deported from the various "operational zones,"[23] the anti-Semitic press became preoccupied with issues relating to the spoliation of Jewish property.

With new and more stringent censorship laws fully enforced after the German occupation, *A Magyar Zsidók Lapja* was also transformed into an instrument of the Nazis and their Hungarian accomplices.[24] As the only "official" organ of Hungarian Jewry—the Jews were urged to subscribe to it—the weekly was exploited by the Nazis to lull the Jews into accepting all the measures that were enacted against them.[25] It printed not only the decrees and orders issued by both the Hungarian and the Nazi authorities, but also the reassuring messages of the central leadership of the Jewish community. The appeals for calm and submission emanating from the leaders of the Jewish Council of Budapest were reinforced by those issued by some of the country's top rabbinical figures. In the virtual absence of any other source of information,[26] the Jewish masses, isolated and uninformed about the realities of Auschwitz, accepted the measures that had been adopted against them. It is one of the great tragedies of the Holocaust era that the provincial Jews of Hungary were liquidated on the eve of Allied victory, when leaders of the world, including the Jewish and non-Jewish leaders of Hungary, were already familiar with the Nazis' Final Solution program. Kept in the dark about the secrets of the death camps, the Hungarian Jews accepted the draconic measures that were enacted against them with the fatalism that characterized the behavior of the other Jewish communities in Nazi-dominated Europe. For the Nazis and their Hungarian accomplices who recognized that the Axis had lost the war against the Allies, the liquidation of Hungarian Jewry represented the last major victory in the genocidal war against the Jews. The anti-Semitic indoctrination and propaganda to which the Hungarian people were subjected during the war years conditioned them to accept the speed, effectiveness and fanaticism with which the deportations were carried out. The genocidal "victory" was made possible not only by the ruthlessness of the SS and the Hungarian gendarmerie and police, but also by the anti-Semitic press.

NOTES

1. Robert E. Conot, *Justice at Nuremberg* (New York: Harper & Row, 1983), pp. 384-85.

2. For some details on the Golden Era of Hungarian Jewry, see Randolph L. Braham, *The Politics of Genocide. The Holocaust in Hungary*, 2d ed. (New York: Columbia University Press, 1994), pp. 1-39. (Cited hereafter as Braham, *Politics*).

3. Under the impact of the depression of the 1930s, the Right radical movements also gained the support of a sizable number of industrial workers and landless peasants who were swayed by the demagogic promises of social and economic reforms.

4. Among the most notorious of these Right-radical journalists were Gábor Bornemissza, Ferenc Fiala, Kálmán Hubay, Károly Maróthy, Ferenc Mikes, István Milotay, Árpád Oláh, Ferenc Rajniss, Oliver Rupprecht, and Ferenc Vajta. For some details on these ultra-Rightist journalists and the newspapers they worked for, consult Róbert Major, *25 év ellenforradalmi sajtó, 1919-1944* (Twenty-Five Years of Counterrevolutionary Press, 1919-1944) (New York: Magyar Zsidók Világszövetsége, 1972).

5. For some details on these Right-radical movements and parties, see Braham, *Politics*, pp. 57-70.

6. Hungary acquired the so-called *Felvidék* (Upper Province) in November 1938, and Carpatho-Ruthenia (*Kárpátalja*) in March 1939, from Czechoslovakia; Northern Transylvania from Romania in August 1940; and the so-called *Délvidék* (Bácska) area from Yugoslavia in April 1941. Its Jewish population, consequently, increased from 400,000 to more than 820,000, including the approximately 100,000 converts identified as Jews under the Nazi laws in effect during the Holocaust.

7. For some specific functions of the Press Division, see below.

8. *Magyar Sajtó* (Hungarian Press), official organ of the Hungarian Press Chamber (*Magyar Sajtókamara*), as quoted by Péter Róbert, *A Holocaust a magyar sajtóban* (The Holocaust in the Hungarian Press), in *Adalékok a magyarországi zsidóság történetéhez* (Contributions to the History of the Jews in Hungary), Randolph L. Braham, ed. (Budapest: Láng Téka, 2000).

9. *Ibid.*, p. 22.

10. Among the journalists drafted into the labor service system were such well-known journalists and writers as Viktor Brassai, Ernö Ligeti, Iván Erdös, Soma Braun, Ernö Salamon, and Béla Zsolt.

11. Among the newspapers banned in Northern Transylvania, for example, were *Új Kelet* (New East), the largest circulation daily published in Kolozsvár (Cluj), and *Népünk* (Our People), published in Nagyvárad (Oradea).

12. Enacted on August 2, 1941, the third anti-Jewish law was clearly based upon the Nuremberg Law of 1935.

13. Historically, many of the Christian denominational journals and periodicals were in the forefront of anti-Judaism and anti-Semitic agitation. Among the worst offenders were the Catholic *Egyházi Közlöny* (Church Gazette) and *Magyar Kultura* (Hungarian Culture). The March 20, 1943 issue of *Magyar Kultura*, the leading periodical of Catholic intellectuals, for example, carried an article by József Takács titled "Krisztus és a zsidóság" (Christ and Jewry). He asserted that the Jews deserved their fate for having murdered Jesus Christ: "The entire people, Jewry as a whole is guilty for this.... Since then they do not constitute a chosen people. Since then there is only a cursed people!" György Kis, *Megjelölve Krisztus keresztjével és Dávid csillagával* (Identified by Christ's Cross and David's Star) (Budapest: The Author, 1987), pp. 228-29. On the anti-Jewish character of Christian press organs, see also pp. 210, 224-25, 229-31, 241, and 254-55. See also Róbert.

14. *A Magyar Zsidók Lapja*, October 11, 1941, p. 2.

15. *Ibid.*

16. The suspension was noted without comment by *A Magyar Zsidók Lapja*. Róbert, *A Holocaust a magyar sajtóban.*

17. Among the most influential local press organs in Trianon Hungary were *Györi Nemzeti Hirlap* (National Journal of Györ), *Debreceni Újság* (Newspaper of Debrecen), *Reggeli Hirlap* (Morning Journal) of Miskolc, and *Dunántul* (Transdanubia), the regional organ.

18. Among the most important local Rightist newspapers in Northern Transylvania, for example, were *Esti Lap* (Evening Journal) of Kolozsvár, *Szamosvölgye* (Szamos Valley) of Dés, the daily *Székely Nép* (The Szekely People) of Sepsiszentgyörgy—the largest provincial paper in Hungary, the weekly *Gyrgyói Lapok* (Gyergyó Papers) of Gyergyószentmiklós, and three Kolozsvár periodicals: *Hitel* (Credit), *Pásztortüz* (Shepherd's Fire), and *Katolikus Status* (Catholic Status).

19. Mihály Kolosváry-Borcsa had previously served as Chief of the Press Department in the Béla Imrédy government (1938-39). He was appointed to this new position on April 7, although the announcement was not made until April 15. *Budapesti Közlöny* (Gazette of Budapest), April 30, 1944, pp. 5-6. He was relieved of the position on September 9, 1944, i.e., two months after the mass deportations were halted.

20. For details on the structure, functions, and personnel of the Press Division, the Hungarian Press Chamber, and the National Press Council during the 1942-44 period, see *Magyarország tiszti cim– és névtára* (Title and Name Register of Hungary) (Budapest:

Magyar Királyi Állami Nyomda), vol. 49, 1942, pp. 26, 32; vol. 50, 1943, pp. 27, 33-34; vol. 51, 1944, pp. 27, 34-35; and vol. 51, 1944 (Supplement), p. 8.

21. Between April 1942 and August 1944 the Propaganda Office was headed by István Antal, who also served as minister of justice and acting minister of religious affairs and education.

22. The founders included Kolosváry-Borcsa, Zoltán Bosnyák, László Endre, and Ákos Doroghi Farkas—notorious anti-Semites who played a leading role in the destruction of Hungarian Jewry.

23. The deportation of the Jews began on May 15, 1944, and by the time it was halted on July 9, all of Hungary (with the notable exception of Budapest) was already *Judenrein*.

24. A short while after the occupation, the name of the weekly was changed to *A Magyarországi Zsidók Lapja* (Journal of the Jews of Hungary). This was in tune with the new political climate in the country that no longer identified the Jews as "Hungarian" but merely as living in Hungary.

25. For some details, see Braham, *Politics*, pp. 462-78.

26. Almost immediately after the occupation, the Jews were prohibited from having radios and telephones, forbidden to travel, and compelled to wear a Yellow Star.

4

The Holocaust in Hungary: An Historical Interpretation of the Role of the Hungarian Radical Right

It is almost universally assumed by historians and laymen alike that the destruction of Hungarian Jewry was solely the consequence of the German occupation of Hungary on March 19, 1944. While it is true that mass deportation of Jews took place only during the occupation, the role played by the Hungarian radical Right[1] in precipitating the catastrophe has been ignored, or at best underestimated in both the general and the Jewish historiography of the postwar period. This article aims to demonstrate the link between the destruction of Hungarian Jewry and the initiatives that were taken by the radical Right of the Hungarian military and political establishment years before the occupation. A closer investigation of the currently available evidence indicates that one of the determining factors underlying the destruction of the Jewish community was the desire of the Hungarian radical Right to rid the country of its "alien" Jews.

Although these elements of the radical Right were relatively unknown and played only a secondary role in the country's military and political establishment, their position on the Jewish question had been accepted by the Nazis immediately concerned with the "Final Solution" as the position of "Hungarian statesmen." Notwithstanding the Hungarian government's official opposition to the "Final Solution," the Nazis looked upon these radical Rightists as pawns to be used for the implementation of their sinister designs in the country.

The category of alien Jews which the radical Right wanted to eliminate consisted basically of the following three groups: (1) The refugees, who had found a haven in Hungary from persecution in Nazi-occupied territories and Slovakia;[2] (2) The Jews of foreign

Reprinted from *Societas*, Vol. 2, No. 3, 1972, pp. 195-220.

background—mostly Galician Jews who had fled to Hungary during World War I—and who had lived there for several decades but been refused naturalization; and (3) A large percentage of the Jews inhabiting the areas which were acquired by Hungary during the 1938-1941 period.[3] Unlike many of their brethren of Trianon Hungary, who tended towards assimilation and acculturation, a large percentage of these Jews refused to identify themselves as "Magyars of the Israelite faith" and continued to cling to their own traditions.

In addition to suffering the consequences of the discriminatory anti-Jewish laws which affected all of Hungary's Jewry since 1938, many of these alien Jews also suffered the crushing burden of poverty and the special police measures that were enacted against them. Nevertheless, they continued to live in relative physical safety until shortly after Hungary's entry into the war against the Soviet Union on June 27, 1941.

However, the ambiguously anti-Semitic policies of Admiral Miklós Horthy's conservative, aristocratic, gentry-dominated, semifascist regime, which starting in 1919 was motivated to a considerable extent by the counterrevolutionary "Szeged Idea" *(A szegedi gondolat)*[4] slipped logically and inevitably toward the open, though at first only partial, adoption of the Nazi solution of the Jewish question. Soon after the outbreak of hostilities, there arose the desire to emulate the Third Reich by transcending the legal solution of the problem of the alien Jews by a *physical* one, which would involve their arrest, internment, and "resettlement."

This solution, at first designed for and successfully employed only against alien Jews, came to be applied three years later against the entire community with almost equal success.

Emboldened by the initial successes of the anti-Soviet military campaign, and reports on the effective "dejudaification" of the occupied territories, a plan for the resettlement of alien Jews in Galicia originated with the KEOKH (*Külföldieket Ellenörzö Országos Központi Hatoság*; National Central Alien Control Office). Empowered to act by the Council of Ministers, the KEOKH began, in July, 1941, a round-up of such Jews, together with a number of Hungarian Jews who could not prove their citizenship. About 15,000 to 18,000 of them were deported, and most of them were subsequently slaughtered by the *SS* and their Hungarian and Ukrainian hirelings near Kamenets Podolsk on August 27-28, 1941.[5]

The success of this first mission encouraged a number of high-ranking military officers and ambitious political figures of the Right to pursue the "purification" of the country of all its alien elements. Disgruntled by Hungary's failure to solve its Jewish question and encouraged by the ever greater pressure on Budapest by the Third Reich, the radical Right decided to take matters into its own hands and entrusted the initiative to those officers. Among the most prominent of them were Major-General József Heszlényi,[6] commander of the Fourth Army Corps, and Lieutenant-General Sándor Homlok,[7] the Hungarian military attaché in Berlin.

Coincidentally, the initiative was undertaken at the time when Hungarian soldiers, led by another group of Germanophile officers headed by General Ferenc Feketehalmy-Czeydner, commander of the Fifth Army Corps of Szeged, were clearing the Novi Sad (Ujvidék) area of "partisans" by killing 3,309 people, among them about 700 Jews.

Acting, presumably without authorization, in the name of the Hungarian government,[8] Heszlényi took the initiative in proposing to the Germans that a second, larger group of alien Jews be deported to the then Rumanian-occupied part of the Soviet Union "east of the Dniester," namely Transnistria. He submitted his proposal to Dr. Karl Clodius, deputy chief of the Economic Policy Division of the German Foreign Office, early in January, 1942. Clodius was quite a familiar figure in Budapest, for he tended to visit Hungary frequently in connection with foreign trade relations between the two countries. Clodius dutifully forwarded the proposal to the OKW (*Oberkommmando der Wehrmacht*) where it was taken up shortly thereafter at a meeting which included the representatives of the *SS* and the Foreign Office in Occupied Eastern Territories. Attractive as the proposal must have appeared, it had to be shelved for a few months—until later in the spring—because of transportation difficulties.[9]

In the interim, the Bárdossy ministry was replaced, on March 7, 1942, by that of Miklós Kállay and the Rightist-inspired deportation project was temporarily allowed to lapse. Kállay's position in connection with the Jewish question was as ambivalent as his general policy. While definitely not a pro-Nazi, and perhaps not even a Germanophile, he was a typical representative of the old, aristocratic-gentry order of Hungary dedicated to the preservation of the status quo.

Although he consistently opposed the physical solution of the Jewish question, he was an advocate of the "civilized" form of anti-Semitism, which aimed, *inter alia*, at the gradual elimination of Jews from the country's economic and intellectual life. And, in fact, with the exception of the atrocities committed against the labor battalion draftees in the Ukraine, who were beyond his immediate control, Jews were not subjected to any mass physical violence during his tenure. However, partially in pursuit of his own political objectives and partially in an attempt to appease the Germans, Kállay exacerbated their legal position and tolerated the virulent anti-Semitic agitation and propaganda, which played into the hands of the Nazis during the occupation.

Kállay's position on the Third Reich, as on the Jewish question in general, tended to fluctuate with the fortunes of the war.[10] While during his first year in office, convinced of Nazi military supremacy,[11] he pursued a consistently pro-German policy, during his second year, that is to say, after the destruction of the Hungarian army at Voronezh on January 12, 1943, and the defeat of the Germans at Stalingrad on February 2, 1943, he began to reorient his policies towards a possible extrication of Hungary from the Axis Alliance.

Although eager to free Hungary from the clutches of Nazism before its final defeat, Kállay, like Horthy and the other representatives of his class, was paralyzed by his fear of Russia and communism. He tried unrealistically to solve his dilemma by maneuvering secretly for the possible surrender of Hungary to the Western Powers exclusively. His naiveté in overlooking the geopolitical realities of the area, the political bases of Anglo-American-Soviet relations, and the military implications of the Grand Alliance was matched by his double-dealing opportunism. Designed to safeguard the integrity of the country and preserve the antiquated social structure of gentry-dominated society, Kállay's policies nevertheless led to disaster. Preoccupied as he was with his efforts to avoid a Soviet occupation, he failed to take the necessary precautionary measures to forestall a possible German attack from without and a pro-Nazi coup from within. It was this vacillating policy and the open courting of the West that induced the Germans to occupy the country in order to prevent it from emulating Italy. The extrication of Hungary at the time the Soviet forces were already crossing the Dniester would have exposed the Nazis in the central and southern parts of Europe to encirclement and possibly to a crushing defeat. The destruction of Hungarian Jewry was to a large extent a concomitant of this German military decision.

Although Kállay was consistently opposed to any physical solution of the Jewish question, he was not, in 1942 at least, politically averse to the advancement of proposals for the "humane" resettlement of the Jews. In a policy statement delivered on April 20, 1942, and calculated to a large extent to appease the pro-Nazi elements at home and abroad just prior to his scheduled visit with Hitler on June 5, Kállay in fact mentioned the desirability of solving the Jewish question in Hungary by expelling the approximately 800,000 Jews who lived there. However, he merely identified this as a goal to be implemented eventually after the war.[12]

In contradistinction to Kállay, some of his military and political subordinates manifested greater impatience on the Jewish question and demanded and worked for an immediate solution. They planned to solve the problem by effectuating the resettlement of the Jews in several phases, with the first installment designed to include 100,000 alien Jews. Thus, about four months after Kállay came into office, the initiative undertaken by Major-General Heszlényi was revived. In the interim, the policies of the new government crystallized; the "Final Solution of the Jewish question" was decided upon at the Wannsee Conference held on January 20, 1942; and many thousands of Hungarian-speaking Jews had already perished together with their Slovakian brethren in Auschwitz.[13]

The initiative for the resettlement of the alien Jews was now assumed by Sándor Homlok. In a letter dated July 2, 1942, he reminded the OKW about the request submitted by Heszlényi and demanded a definitive solution.[14] Towards the end of the same month, Karl Klingenfuss, legation counselor in the *Deutschland* (later *Inland*) section of the German Foreign Office, expressed his section's concurrence with Hungary's desire to get rid of its unwanted Jews and promised to look into the problem of transportation, which had prevented the implementation of the plan by OKW in January. He also promised to investigate the feasibility of using Transnistria as the destination for the deportees.[15] Early in August, he informed the OKW that the entire matter was being transferred for a final decision to the RSHA (*Reichssicherheitshauptamt*; Reich Security Main Office), Heinrich Himmler's agency in charge of resettlements.[16] Since Himmler's resettlement areas, such as Auschwitz and Treblinka, were in German-occupied Poland, Klingenfuss hastened to inform, on August 5, 1942, Adolf Eichmann about the good news that the Rumanians had shelved the idea of transferring the Hungarian Jews to the "area between the Bug and Moldavia."[17]

The project gathered momentum and on September 17, Klingenfuss again communicated with Eichmann informing him that the Wehrmacht representative, a certain Major Wiesner, was anxious to have the response of the RSHA, for the case was to be taken up at a conference to be held some time at the end of the same month.[18] In his letter of September 25, 1942, Eichmann, citing technical reasons, rejected the idea of mobilizing the entire deportation apparatus merely for the expulsion of the Jewish refugees. He contended that it would be better to delay this action until Hungary was ready to bring about the total solution of the Jewish question.[19] Klingenfuss relayed this answer to the OKW on September 30.[20]

The scheme to bring about the resettlement of 100,000 Jews as a first installment of the solution of the Jewish question in Hungary was known not only to the higher German authorities and generals Heszlényi and Homlok, but, as the evidence clearly shows, also to a number of leading Hungarian political figures. György Ottlik, a member of the influential Foreign Affairs Committee of the Upper House of Parliament and the chief editor of the German-language newspaper *Pester Lloyd* of Budapest, the semiofficial organ of the government, visited Germany in the course of his West European tour made during August and September, 1942. Upon his return he submitted, on October 10, a lengthy memorandum to the Foreign Ministry, then headed by Prime Minister Kállay. Based on a three-hour conversation he had had with Sztójay, the Hungarian minister in Berlin, during the first day of his visit to the German capital, the memorandum reveals that Sztójay knew about the German decision to solve the Jewish question in a radical manner during the course of the war. Ottlik further contended that, according to Sztójay, only two elements strained Hungarian-German relations: One was the Hungarian attitude towards the German *Volksgruppe* living in the country—a problem which was being solved. The other, to quote Sztójay's statement to Ottlik, was "the incomparably graver one, the great influence and role played by the Jews in Hungary." The memorandum continues:

> As long as this is condoned, one cannot trust in the Hungarians. Sztójay consequently would find it appropriate if Hungary did not wait until (the Germans) raised this issue sharply, but would expedite the tempo of the changing of the guards and resettle a sizeable portion of our Jewish population in occupied Russia. Our Minister first spoke of about 300,000[21] but then bargained himself down to 100,000. On my interjected remark he did not keep it a secret that resettlement meant execution.[22]

About the same time, that is, in early October, 1942, *SS-Hauptsturmführer* Dieter Wisliceny, then serving in Bratislava and in charge of the deportation of Slovak Jews, visited Budapest. In his report to Hans Elard Ludin, the German minister in Bratislava, dated October 8, 1942, Wisliceny stated that two days earlier he had been introduced to a certain Fáy, whom he identified as Kállay's personal secretary.[23] The introduction was effectuated by Dr. Gábor Szarka, secretary of the Hungarian Chamber of Foreign Trade in Bratislava.[24]

As a person in charge of economic matters, Szarka probably knew and dealt with Augustín Morávek, the head of UHU (*Ustredny Hospodarsky Urad*; Central Office for Economy). UHU was founded in 1940, and operated under the immediate jurisdiction of the Prime Minister of Slovakia. This agency was vested, *inter alia,* with complete authority relating to the elimination of Jews from the economic and social life of the country and the transfer of their property to Aryans. It was in Morávek's office, moreover, that negotiations for the resettlement of the Jews of Slovakia were launched in May, 1941, with the participation of Wisliceny, who was officially appointed by the Slovak authorities as "Adviser for UHU," and of Dr. Erich Gebert, the adviser to the Ministry of Economy and Finance.[25]

By the time Wisliceny paid his visit to Budapest, close to 58,000 Slovak Jews, or about seventy-five percent of the community, had already been deported to Auschwitz.[26] By then he clearly deserved the designation of "expert" on the Final Solution of the Jewish question. Concerned with this yet unsolved problem in Hungary, Szarka must have been impressed with Wisliceny's accomplishments when he introduced him to Fáy.

In his report to Ludin, Wisliceny states that immediately after lunch at the Golf Club in the Svábhegy section of Budapest on October 6, Fáy inquired closely about the solution of the Jewish question in Slovakia and solicited his (Wisliceny's) views on the question in Hungary. The report continues:

> Fáy mentioned that the existing laws were inadequate and that the concept of Jews was also not specified in sufficiently clear form. The economic 'dejudaification' was also said not to have led to the desired results. The problem was very difficult, since the Jews represented an enormous economic factor and their large number also was important. A resettlement of the Jews from Hungary, as was being carried out at this time in all Europe, could be realized only in stages [in Hungary]. Fáy asked me whether it was a fact that the Jews were being resettled out of Rumania as well. I answered him that to my knowledge preparations to that effect were being made. Suddenly Fáy asked if Hungary would also be considered in a resettlement program. It was a matter of about 100,000 Jews in Carpatho-Ukraine and the territories acquired from Rumania, which Hungary would like to resettle. As a second stage, one would have to handle the [Jews in the Hungarian Plains], and finally [those in] the capital city of Budapest. I then told him that I was in Budapest merely for private reasons and that I could not answer this question. I had no clear picture whether there were reception possibilities for Hungarian Jews in the Eastern Territories. I had the impression that Fáy had tried to make my acquaintance through Szarka and that he asked these questions on higher orders.[27]

This document is extremely important, for it not only identifies for the first time the intended composition of the first 100,000 Jews to be resettled, namely Jews from Carpatho-Ruthenia and Northern Transylvania, but also reveals that it was designed merely as the first of several phases of the resettlement program calculated to bring about the total solution of the Jewish question in Hungary.

It is not clear whether the resettlement idea originated with Fáy or Szarka or some other Hungarian Nazis like the notorious Jew-baiters László Baky, László Endre, or Baron László Vay acting singly or in concert with the military establishment. It is safe to assume, however, that it was advanced without the knowledge or consent of Prime Minister Kállay. Wisliceny's statement to the effect that it was his impression that Fáy asked his questions "on higher orders" cannot be accepted as hardcore evidence.

Ludin dutifully forwarded Wisliceny's report to the German Foreign Office with a covering letter dated October 13.[28] It must have reached the RSHA shortly thereafter, for Himmler himself suddenly took a personal interest in the affair. He approached Joachim von Ribbentrop, the Foreign Minister of the Third Reich, in a lengthy letter dated November 30, 1942, in which he reviewed the Heszlényi offer to the OKW as expressed in the name of the Hungarian government. He further reminded him of the recent demands advanced by Hungarian statesmen for the solution of the Jewish question in that nation. Almost paraphrasing Fáy's assertion as stated in Wisliceny's report, Himmler informed Ribbentrop that the solution of the Jewish question in Hungary was envisioned to be carried out in several phases, with the first phase to involve the evacuation of 100,000 Jews from the eastern part of the country. He stressed that although at first he had been against a partial solution of the question in Hungary, he was now ready to assign Wisliceny, the expert responsible for clearing Slovakia of its Jews, to the German legation in Budapest, where he could act as a "scientific adviser." Himmler further claimed that the elimination of this "burning problem" in Hungary would undoubtedly also affect the Bulgarian and Rumanian governments inducing them to solve their respective Jewish questions as well.[29]

At Ribbentrop's request,[30] Martin Luther, the chief of the *Deutschland* section of the German Foreign Office, instructed Dietrich von Jagow, the German minister in Budapest, to inquire whether the Hungarian authorities were ready to effectuate the deportation of the 100,000 alien Jews or perhaps all of the Jews of Hungary.[31] In his answer of February 18, 1943, Jagow informed the Foreign Office that he had instructed the German military attaché in Budapest to contact the Hungarian General Staff and ascertain whether Heszlényi and Homlok were actually empowered by their government to make the request for the deportation of the alien Jews. The text of Jagow's final report remains a mystery, for the archives of the German Foreign Office contain no record of it.[32]

The Hungarian initiative announced by Wisliceny, however, received new impetus revealing the sinister role played by Baron László Vay in the solution of the Jewish question. Vay was a leading member of the Rightist radical wing of *MÉP (Magyar Élet Pártja*; Party of Hungarian Life), the government party, which he headed until November, 1940, when Béla Lukács, another member of the same wing, took over leadership. A former prefect of Debrecen and Hajdú County (1935), Vay was also a member of the Foreign Affairs Committee and of the Public Administration Committee of the Upper House of Parliament (1942).[33] He was one of the prominent members of the Lukács-led Hungarian delegation,[34] which visited *Reichsleiter* Martin Bormann, the chief of the Nazi Party Chancellery, in Munich on March 12, 1943. About two weeks before his departure, Vay sought out Jagow and expressed his hope that the Jewish question would also be discussed in Munich, "for there was much to be done yet in this area in Hungary." He was particularly anxious that Lukács and his colleagues be briefed on this question in depth and in an authoritative fashion. Jagow alerted the Foreign Office that the initiative must not be revealed as having come from Vay.[35]

In response to this initiative, Bergmann, a minister in the *Inland* section of the Foreign Office, prepared with Ribbentrop's concurrence a lengthy memorandum dated March 9, 1943, to guide Bormann in his discussion with Lukács and his colleagues. Specifically, the Hungarian government was to be advised: (1) To exclude all Jews forthwith and without exception by appropriate legislation from the country's intellectual and economic life and to dispossess them immediately without compensation; (2) To mark all Jews without delay in order to facilitate governmental measures against them and to enable the [Hungarian] people to hold themselves aloof from them; and (3) To concur with the prompt beginning of the deportation and transportation [of the Jews] to the East by the appropriate German organization.[36]

It was at this time that the Regent, Horthy, was extended an invitation to visit Hitler at Schloss Klessheim, near Salzburg. At the meeting, which took place on April 17, 1943, the Regent was advised by the Führer that Hungary ought to follow the example of Poland where "if the Jews did not want to work they were simply shot." Upon Horthy's alleged assertion that he could not have Jews killed after they were deprived of a livelihood, Ribbentrop, who also attended the conference, replied that they should "either be killed or sent to concentration camps."[37] Ribbentrop's views on the Jewish question were further detailed by Sztójay in a lengthy memorandum dated April 28, in which he proposed that this problem "should be solved in a way that will avert a third [German] intervention."[38]

About a month later, on May 21, Sztójay was already in a position to inform Horst Wagner, Luther's successor as chief of the *Inland II* section of the German Foreign Office, that in the wake of the Hitler-Horthy discussions on the Jewish question at Klessheim, Kállay was about "to consider seriously the initiation of decisive measures against the Jews." Sztójay also pointed out the difficulties underlying the solution of the question in Hungary and suggested that the anti-Jewish measures be implemented gradually and at first involve the resettlement of only a part of the Jews who, in order not to alarm the ones left behind, should be allowed for a short while to earn a living for themselves."[39]

There is reason to believe, however, that Sztójay did not convey the official position of the government at the time. In responding to a request by the Foreign Office, Jagow in fact informed his superiors on June 2, 1943 that he personally doubted that Sztójay was authorized to make his statement to Wagner. Kállay's position, according to Jagow, was reiterated in his speech of May 29, 1943, in which he stated that he was not inclined to deport Jews as long as he did not know where to relocate them.[40]

But by this time, four months after the Voronezh and Stalingrad disasters, the Prime Minister was already groping, however unrealistically, for an honorable way out of the war. The search for peace gathered momentum after Italy's surrender late in the summer and in consequence of the military victories of the Anglo-American forces in Italy, North Africa, and the Far East, and the inexorable advance of the Red Army in eastern Europe. The establishment of contacts with representatives of the Western Allies was accompanied in fact by a relative easing of the position of the Jews, which was felt especially by those in the labor battalions. But while Kállay became increasingly involved in his inauspicious secret negotiations, he, like Horthy on October 15, 1944, failed to take the most elementary military precautionary measures. The General Staff, like the officer corps on the whole, continued to be composed almost exclusively of Germanophiles of Homlok's and Heszlényi's ilk, and the press with a few exceptions continued to feed the anti-Jewish psychosis that preoccupied the people. Because of Hungary's strategic position and Hitler's well-based fear of another impending Italian-type surrender, the German General Staff finalized the plans for the country's occupation as early as September 1943.[41] The actual invasion, however, took place on March 19, 1944, during Horthy's second visit to Klessheim.

In the interim, Hitler's suspicions were reinforced by a lengthy memorandum that Edmund Veesenmayer, an SS Brigadier General who later became the German minister and Reich plenipotentiary in Budapest, sent to the German Foreign Office in December 1943,[42] and by Horthy's demand made on February 12, 1944, that Hungarian troops be withdrawn from the eastern front in order to make possible the "defense of the Hungarian frontiers.[43]

Veesenmayer presented a very bleak picture of Hungary's performance as an ally and submitted a series of proposals to correct the situation. The changes were to be brought about by keeping Horthy in power in spite of his weaknesses. Veesenmayer was not far from the mark when he characterized the Regent as basically a good soldier, but "a miserable politician," who "understands nothing about either domestic or foreign policy."

Portending the German occupation, Veesenmayer suggested that the Hungarian problem would be solved, for all practical intents and purposes, if Horthy were freed from his entourage and "made a soldier of the *Führer.*" He called for the replacement of Horthy's advisers by the *Führer*, the Reich, and a delegate of the Reich "who is up to his mission." In connection with the Jewish question in Hungary, he contended that "the Jews are enemy No. 1 and the 1.1 million Jews amount to as many saboteurs...and will have to be looked upon as Bolshevik vanguards."

After a stormy encounter with the *Führer* on March 18, Horthy and his entourage left Klessheim with no written agreement but with Hitler's assurances that German troops would leave Hungary as soon as an acceptable government was formed and that no satellite, that is Croatian, Rumanian, or Slovak, troops would be involved in the occupation. However, the assurances did not specifically include the withdrawal of SS units. Although no formal agreement was signed at Klessheim,[44] there is absolutely no doubt that the question of the treatment of the Jews was also discussed and that Horthy made certain concessions that proved disastrous for them.

In his report to the Crown Council, which was convened shortly after his return on March 19, the Regent made no reference to these concessions, but merely reported Hitler's complaint that "Hungary did nothing in the matter of the Jewish problem, and was not prepared to settle accounts with the large Jewry in Hungary." In this connection, he also quoted Hitler's assertion with reference to the Jews of Finland. The *Führer* allegedly said: "Finland had only 6,000 Jews and what a subversive activity even these carried out against Finland further standing her ground."[45] Laconic as the report was on the Jewish question, the minutes of the Crown Council meeting clearly reveal that the Regent, while anticipating many German demands, considered the Nazi occupation less of an evil than a possible Russian invasion.

It appears that either Horthy deliberately failed to inform the Crown Council about the agreement to supply Germany with Jewish workers or that the Council decided not to record this obviously controversial item in the minutes. The evidence, however, reveals that he in fact did agree—however reluctantly and most probably under great pressure—to the delivery of a considerable number of "Jewish workers for German war production purposes." The Regent's concurrence was important to the Germans who were eager to assure the cooperation of the new, pro-Nazi government and to provide legitimacy for the limited anti-Jewish operation.

Hitler had no difficulty in demonstrating his needs. The Germans were suffering terrible losses on the eastern front and the aircraft industry was heavily damaged by the American Eighth and Fifteenth Air Forces. Field Marshall Erhard Milch, then state secretary in the Air Ministry and armaments chief of the *Luftwaffe*, approached Albert

Speer, Minister of Armaments and War Production, on February 23, 1944, with the idea that a Fighter Aircraft Staff be established for purposes of pooling the talents and resources of their two ministries "in order to overcome the crisis in aircraft production."[46] The plan, as worked out in detail by Xavier Dorsch, a department head in Speer's ministry, called for the construction of six underground industrial plants, each with an area of over one million square feet, to be completed by November 1944. One of these was to be built in the Protectorate of Bohemia and Moravia with the aid of Jewish workers from Hungary. To head the Fighter Aircraft Staff, Hitler appointed Karl Saur, a department chief in the Armaments Ministry of whom Milch and Speer also approved.[47]

On March 18, 1944, the day Horthy visited Hitler, Speer was convalescing in the Cloverleaf Palace, a curved pavilion in the park of Schloss Klessheim.[48] The immediate labor needs for the project in the Protectorate were presumably discussed in light of Speer's communication and of the Hungarian statesmen's earlier offers relating to 100,000 Jews. In fact, Hitler and Speer again reviewed the manpower needs of the *Jägerstab* project in the first week of April, and agreed to request that the 100,000 Jews be sent from Hungary.[49] In response to this review and Horthy's apparent concurrence, Hitler informed Milch on April 9 that 100,000 Hungarian Jews "were to be found for the construction of underground aircraft factories in the Reich."[50]

Duly appointed to his new position, Saur called a top-secret meeting of the Fighter Aircraft Staff on April 14, 1944, and revealed that the details relating to the employment of 100,000 Hungarian Jews in the Protectorate project were being finalized by Schlempp and Schmelter, who were working under Dorsch.[51] On the same day, Veesenmayer informed Ribbentrop that Sztójay had given him a "binding assurance" that 50,000 able-bodied Jews would be placed at the disposal of the Reich by the end of the same month, and that 50,000 more would be made available before the end of May. He further reported that practical measures for the implementation of Sztójay's assurances were already under way through the action initiated by the *SD (Sicherheitsdienst*; Security Service) and the Hungarian police. He also revealed that he had the concurrence of the Regent and that the *Honvédség* (Hungarian Armed Forces) and the

Ministry of the Interior had expressed their readiness to cooperate.[52] The following day, Veesenmayer reported to the German Foreign Office that the *Honvédség* was ready to provide 5,000 Jews at once, to be followed by an additional 5,000 every three or four days until the figure of 50,000 was reached. With the Jews now at his disposal, Veesenmayer asked for instructions as to where in Germany the transports should be directed.[53]

The news about the availability of Hungarian Jews was immediately relayed to Eichmann.[54] Veesenmayer pressed for freight cars,[55] and was assured that all the details relating to the time and means of shipping them were being worked out by the RSHA in close cooperation with Eichmann and his staff and Ernst Kaltenbrunner.[56]

In the meantime, the newly established government headed by Sztójay issued a series of anti-Jewish decrees, including one requiring Jews to wear the distinctive yellow Star of David while the Jewish Council, which was established under the order of and for a while made responsible exclusively to the Germans, was busy organizing the Jewish community on a national basis.

The northeastern parts of the country, namely Carpatho-Ruthenia and Transylvania, were declared "operational zones" on April 13, and three days later, on the eve of Passover, the Jews of Carpatho-Ruthenia were rounded up as a "precautionary measure." They were driven into ghettos about two weeks before the actual "ghettoization" decree was promulgated on April 28.[57] The plans for their deportation were being finalized in accordance with a decision of the Council of Ministers of April 26, under which 50,000 labor service men were authorized to be sent to Germany together with their families.[58]

On April 29, Veesenmayer reported that the first transport, including 1,800 able-bodied Jews between the ages of 16 and 50, had been shipped from Budapest (Kistarcsa) and that 2,000 more would be sent from Topolya the following day.[59]

This transport of April 29, then, was the first installment in meeting the Germans' *bona fide* demand for 100,000 Jews based on: (1) Horthy's and the Hungarian government's concurrence with the shipment of Jews to Germany; (2) Germany's military construction needs in the Protectorate; and (3) The original Heszlényi-Homlok-Fáy offers. Although the minutes of the Crown Council meeting of March

19 are silent on the subject, the record clearly shows that Horthy agreed to the shipment of Jews to Germany.[60]

According to Ribbentrop, who attended the Klessheim Conference and dealt closely with both Horthy and Sztójay, the Regent agreed that "a considerable number of Jewish workers were to be made available for German war production."[61] Otto Winkelmann, a high officer in the *SS*, and Himmler's immediate representative in Hungary in 1944, stated in the Ministries Trial that there was a "legal agreement" with the Hungarian government "for the deportation of what was initially 100,000 Jews."[62] This was also corroborated by *SS-Hauptsturmführer* Ernst Kienast, Winkelmann's assistant in Budapest, who testified that according to his superior "the necessity for a solution of the Jewish question in Hungary was unequivocally established by Hitler at Klessheim and urgently pressed through," although "no agreement was reached on the form which the solution should take, nor on the extent of the program."[63]

In his testimony during his trial in 1948, Veesenmayer stated:

> Horthy himself told me that he was interested only in protecting the prosperous, the economically valuable Jews in Budapest, those who were well off. However, as to the remaining Jewry—and he used a very ugly term there—he had no interest in them and was quite prepared to have them go to the Reich or elsewhere for labor. He approved that; and he did not approve it after a demand made by me but he approved it after agreements and discussions with his premier and his ministries. The fact has been proved that he later—at first he moderated the deportations, and then later stopped them. Somebody who forbids something later on, must have given permission for it earlier.[64]

This assessment of Horthy was also corroborated by László Baky. In his statement written while in prison, Baky claimed that he had issued the decree of April 7, 1944, which called for the "ghettoization" of Jews, because László Endre, state secretary in charge of political (that is, Jewish) affairs in the Ministry of the Interior, and as such one of those chiefly responsible for the destruction of the Jews, had requested it on the basis that "the Regent agreed to the delivery of the Jews to the Germans for purposes of labor."[65] He believed this, he claimed, because during his own previous audience with the Regent, Horthy had told him:

> Baky, you are one of my old Szeged officers. The Germans have cheated me. Now they want to deport the Jews. I don't mind. I hate the Galician Jews and the Communists. Out with them, out of the country! But you must see, Baky, that there are some Jews who are as good Hungarians as you and I. For example, here are little Chorin and Vida—aren't they good Hungarians? I can't allow these to be taken away. But they can take the rest.[66]

Baky's identification of Horthy's attitude towards the Jews was also corroborated by Haller, Veesenmayer's secretary. In his view "Horthy considered the assimilated Jews of Budapest as Hungarians, but the poorer ones of the provinces only as rabble for whom he had done nothing for a long time."[67]

Endre also stated in his testimony that "the Regent raised no objection to the deportations, saying that the sooner the operation was concluded, the sooner the Germans would leave the country."[68] Perhaps the most convincing evidence for Horthy's consent was offered by Bishop László Ravasz. He claimed that when he was informed about the atrocities committed during the "ghettoization" in Carpatho-Ruthenia by Zsigmond Perényi, president of the Upper House of Parliament,[69] he contacted Horthy to express his misgivings. At a meeting held on April 28, the Regent told him that "a large number of labor draftees were requested of Hungary.... A few hundred thousand Jews will in this manner leave the country's frontier, but not a single hair of their heads will be touched, just as is the case with the many hundreds of thousands of Hungarian laborers, who have been working in Germany since the beginning of the war."[70]

An unidentified official spokesman of the government, commenting on the deportations, informed foreign journalists in June as follows:

> The Hungarian authorities have placed Jewish manpower at the disposal of the Reich in order to meet the wish [for labor] of the German ally in the interest of the joint conduct of the war, without prejudicing Hungarian war production. It is therefore a question not of deportation but of normal transfer of labor.[71]

This statement was in accord with Sztójay's memorandum of June 26, 1944, cabled to Hungarian diplomatic representatives abroad, which aimed to explain the deportations. It stated:

> In view of the position of the labor market in Hungary as well as of the full share this country takes in the war, the government has not been able to raise the contingent of Hungarian workers for Germany but has wished to comply with the requests of the Germans by placing Jews at their disposal. It was on the grounds of this agreement that Jews were sent to Germany for work. Experiences having proved that in foreign countries the Jews' willingness to work diminishes when they are separated from their families, the members of their families were sent along with them.[72]

One may also mention the conclusion on this matter of Professor C. A. Macartney, the noted expert on Hungary, who cannot be accused of being unsympathetic to the country or to Horthy. In discussing Veesenmayer's request for 50,000 Jewish workers, Macartney very correctly identified it as "an entirely bona fide demand ... [since] Horthy had already, at Klessheim, agreed to supply the Reich with Jewish labor."[73] With the green light provided by the legal agreement under which Horthy and his government consented to the delivery of one hundred thousand or several hundred thousands of Jews to Germany "for war production purposes," the Nazi elements—both German and Hungarian—who saw in this merely the first of several phases in the total solution of the Jewish question in Hungary involving not only the alien but also the assimilated Jews, got busy to take full advantage of the opportunity.

The master plan for the total solution of the Jewish question in Hungary was worked out at the RSHA with the direct involvement of Himmler, Kaltenbrunner, and Eichmann and his staff. It was based, *inter alia,* on the Heszlényi-Homlok-Fáy idea as detailed in Himmler's letter to Ribbentrop of November 30, 1942 and on Germany's immediate needs for labor. On the Hungarian side, it involved the wholehearted cooperation of the ultra-Rightist elements of the Sztójay government and above all of those associated with the Ministry of the Interior, Baky, Endre, and Andor Jaross, who became Minister on March 22, 1944, and had immediate control over the state apparatus and the instruments of coercion: the police and the *gendarmerie*. Baky, Endre, and their immediate collaborators were briefed by Kaltenbrunner, who arrived in Hungary together with Horthy on March 19, and was instrumental in their appointment.

In the finalization of the master plan, the German and the Hungarian leaders had to consider: (1) The rapid advance of the Soviet forces in eastern Europe; (2) The limited German forces available for the operation;[74] (3) The necessity of acquiring the Hungarian government's help to carry out the operation; (4) The desirability to lull the large Jewish community into a false sense of security and optimism in order to minimize the risk of resistance and to induce its leadership to collaborate; and (5) The need to implement the plan with lightning speed.

The scenario as worked out by those directly involved in the operation called for a two-pronged approach: (1) The legal, political, formalistic one to provide the facade of the *bona fide* actions authorized by Horthy and the German and the Hungarian governments; and (2) The covert, technical operation based on the master plan. Each of the many elements and agencies involved—German, Hungarian, and Jewish—had and was to play a preassigned role, though this was not known to many of them at the time.

To satisfy the requirements of the former, Horthy was to remain in office to provide legitimacy; Veesenmayer and his staff were to provide the camouflage of international law; the Hungarian government was to provide the civil service, the police, and the *gendarmerie* to make possible the satisfaction of "Germany's legitimate labor needs" and the clearing of "military operational zones" of potential "saboteurs"; the Jewish Council was to be induced to collaborate by organizing the entire Jewish community and by exercising sole leadership over it; and, last but not least, the Hungarian masses, already mesmerized by decades of anti-Semitic propaganda, were to be persuaded that, finally, their "legitimate" demands were being fulfilled.

The covert, technical operational plan called for the: (1) Separation of Jews from the rest of the population by marking them by means of the compulsory wearing of the yellow Star of David; (2) Expropriation of their property; (3) Their systematic and accelerated internment and deportation to be effectuated on a territorial basis; (4) Deportation was to be requested by the Hungarian authorities "in view of the danger of epidemics and other hardships in the overcrowded ghettos"; (5) Lulling of the Jewish masses into submission in order to avoid the repetition of the Warsaw Ghetto uprising by trapping the leadership into unintended collaboration through a variety of reassurances and rescue and emigration schemes;[75] and (6) Total silence of the press and other media of mass communication concerning the deportations.

In accordance with this scenario, Veesenmayer's earlier request as to where in Germany the transports of Jewish laborers should be sent was duly answered by the RSHA on April 24.[76] As relayed to Veesenmayer on April 27, the reply revealed the objection of the *Sipo (Sicherheitspolizei*; Security Police) and SD chief, Ernst Kaltenbrunner, to the direct assignment of Jews to work in German factories, because that would render Germany's cleansing of Jews "illusory." He saw no objection, however, to their transportation to the labor camps operating under the jurisdiction of the *Reichsführer-SS,* that is, to the concentration camps.[77]

The master plan, in other words, called for the selection of able-bodied Jews for labor in the Reich only after the mass arrival of the deportees in Auschwitz. As Veesenmayer stated in his telegram of May 8, 1944, the "100,000 Hungarian workers required by the Todt Organization for labor allocation in the Reich would have to be requested from the SS Main Administrative and Economic Office *[SS-Gruppenführer* Richard Glücks], which is in charge of Jews to be deported from Hungary."[78]

Under the plan worked out by the RSHA, the 100,000 able-bodied Jews represented about ten percent of the 1,000,000 Jews the Nazis expected to deport from Hungary. It was this percentage target that most probably guided Dr. Josef Mengele and the other "physicians" on the Auschwitz railway station ramp when they made their selections upon the arrival of the transports. The ninety percent casualty rate was corroborated by Rudolf Höss, the former commandant of Auschwitz, who asserted that about 400,000 Hungarian Jews were "executed...at Auschwitz in the summer of 1944."[79]

These documents clearly reveal that the German demands were advanced to satisfy both the manpower needs of the Reich and, above all, the implementation of the ideological grand design of the Nazis for the total and final solution of the Jewish question in Europe before the end of the war. They reveal, in other words, that the Jews were being shipped to German-held territories not so much to work, but primarily to be exterminated.[80]

The master plan was carried out with lightning speed thanks to the unique combination of Germanic efficiency and Hungarian brutality. Within three months the provinces were cleared of Jews by means of the deportation to Auschwitz of 437,402 persons[81]—a sordid record of slaughter, which is unparalleled in the entire annals of human history in terms of magnitude, speed, and technical efficiency.[82]

As the currently available evidence clearly proves, the destruction of Hungarian Jewry was the consequence of both the German occupation and the initiatives taken by and the wholehearted cooperation of the radical Right elements in the country. The speed and efficiency with which the Final Solution was implemented are explained by the high priority the Germans attached to the military projects, which were envisioned to employ 100,000 Jewish workers from Hungary. It appears that the figure of 100,000 was based upon the offer the Hungarian Right, advanced through Heszlényi, Homlok, and Fáy since January 1942, and to whose delivery Horthy agreed apparently under pressure at Klessheim in March 1944. It is probable that the Germans would have been satisfied with the delivery of 100,000 able-bodied Jewish workers, had the Hungarians—like the Bulgarians and Rumanians, not to speak of the Danes and Italians—resisted the total solution of the Jewish question, which, of course, the Nazis preferred. But the first and foremost objective of the Germans in Hungary in 1944 was to keep the Magyars in line and to exploit to the maximum the country's military and economic resources in the death struggle of the Reich with the Grand Alliance. A great share of the responsibility for the extermination of the Jews must therefore be borne by the Magyars themselves. In the words of Jenö Lévai, the noted Hungarian Jewish journalist and one of the foremost experts on the Holocaust in Hungary:

> Owing to their insignificant numbers, the Nazis were practically unable even to supervise the deportations, let alone to carry them out. The marking of the Jews with the Star of David, their "roundup" into

> ghettos and concentration camps, were made possible only by the fact that the gendarmerie—although well-acquainted with the situation and numbering some 20,000 men—could everywhere be sure of the aid of the local police. Even then the procedure could not have been carried through if the Christian population had shown resistance. Thus it must be assumed that, quite apart from the part played by the Regent and the Sztójay Government, the chief causes for the complete sellout of the Jews were the anti-Semitic propaganda with which the Hungarian population had been inundated for scores of years, the stirring up of their hatred and, last but not least, the rousing of the rabble's rapacious instincts.[83]

Veesenmayer was basically correct, then, when he confessed after the war that:

> Had the Hungarians consistently refused to meet the German demands concerning the solution of the Jewish question, this could not have taken place! There would certainly have been "pressure," but as 1944 was already a year of "crisis," we would not have had sufficient power to bring about the roundup and deportation of 1,000,000 people. This is such a grandiose police task that it could have been implemented within three months only with the total and enthusiastic support of the entire military and administrative apparatus. We could not have brought in suitable forces from outside, for this job could be performed only by those who knew the country, its people, and spoke its language. Eichmann had only a small staff. The deportation could be effectuated so quickly and so smoothly only with the total help of the Hungarian Government.[84]

Nevertheless, one must keep in mind that the military and administrative apparatus, which Veesenmayer correctly identified as having enthusiastically supported the deportation program, was provided by the government which he and his Nazi colleagues imposed upon Hungary in the wake of the occupation. Consequently, first and foremost responsibility for the destruction of Hungarian Jewry must rest with the Germans, for while the Hungarian radical Rightists were eager to solve the Jewish question and wholeheartedly collaborated in the deportation program, their plans could not have been carried out in the absence of the occupation.

NOTES

1. This study does not aim to trace the genesis of anti-Semitism in Hungary or to analyze the role played in the destruction of Hungarian Jewry by the many secret or semi-secret "patriotic" associations, such as the Association of Awakening Hungarians (*Ebredö Magyarok Egyesülete*), Hungarian Association of National Defense (*Magyar Országos Véderö Egyesület*), Etelköz Association (*Etelközi Szövetség*) and by the several national socialist movements and parties that flourished in the 1930's and 1940's. It aims primarily to trace the links between the first concrete proposals advanced by certain elements of the Hungarian radical Right toward the solution of the Jewish question and the destruction of the Jewish community after the German occupation of the country on March 19, 1944. It should be borne in mind that these elements acted without the knowledge of, and often in opposition to, the government.

2. The number of Jewish refugees in Hungary at the start of the war (June, 1941) was between 30,000 and 35,000. In the wake of the Kamenets Podolsk massacres, the number was reduced to about 15,000 by November, 1943. Ernest Landau (ed.), *Der Kastner-Bericht über Eichmanns Menschenhandel in Ungarn* (Munich, 1961), p. 45. Slovakia established its independence with the assistance of the Third Reich on March 14, 1939, and almost immediately began to emulate its ally on the Jewish question.

3. In November, 1938, Hungary acquired the so-called Upper Province (Felvidék), including the southern part of Slovakia, with 67,876 Jews; in March, 1939, Hungary forcibly incorporated Carpatho-Ruthenia or Sub-Carpathia (Kárpátalja) with 78,087 Jews; in August, 1940, Hungary obtained Northern Transylvania (Eszak Erdély) with 164,052 Jews; and in April, 1941, conquered the Backa (Bácska) and the adjacent areas of Yugoslavia with 14,202 Jews. Ernö László, "Hungary's Jewry: A Demographic Overview, 1918-1945," *Hungarian-Jewish Studies*, Randolph L. Braham, ed., (New York, 1969), II, 137-182. Hungarians understandably resentful of the Trianon and other post-World War I agreements insist that these territories were regained rather than acquired, since they had been part of Hungary before the war.

4. The "Szeged Idea" denotes basically the somewhat nebulous philosophy and program of the Right radicals and counterrevolutionaries, who rallied around Admiral Miklós Horthy in the city of Szeged, then (1918-1919) under French occupation. Aside from its conservative-fascist component, the idea also incorporated a virulent form of anti-Semitism fostered by the propagandistic identification of Jewry with Bolshevism. The main supporters of the idea included the fixed-income middle and lower middle classes that were hard hit by the inflationary pressures of the post-war period, army officers of the disintegrated Hungarian Army, and refugee-bureaucrats from the territories ceded to the Successor States (Czechoslovakia, Rumania, and Yugoslavia).

5. For further details on the Kamenets Podolsk massacre see Arthur Geyer, "Az elsö magyarországi deportálás" (The First Hungarian Deportation), in *Uj Élet Naptár, 1960-1961* (New Life Calendar, 1960-1961) (Budapest, 1960), pp. 75-82; and Randolph L. Braham, "The Kamenets Podolsk and Délvidék Massacres: Prelude to the Holocaust in Hungary," in *Yad Vashem Studies*, Livia Rothkirchen, ed. (Jerusalem, 1972), IX.

6. Very little verifiable biographical data is available on Heszlényi. In 1942, he was the head of Section III of the Ministry of Defense in charge of supplies and procurement. *Magyarország tiszti cim — és névtára* (Title and Name Register of Hungary) (Budapest, 1942), IL, 628. It is most probably in this capacity that he came into contact with Dr. Karl

Clodius, deputy chief of the Economic Policy Division of the German Foreign Office. Recognized as one of the leading Germanophile officers, he was recommended on May 13, 1944, by Edmund Veesenmayer, German Minister and Reich Plenipotentiary in Hungary, as the best possible candidate for the position of Deputy Minister of Defense. Veesenmayer identified him as "one of the best officers enjoying great prestige in the army," who "is unimpeachable from the political point of view." György Ránki, et al., eds. and comps., *A Wilhelmstrasse és Magyarország. Német diplomáciai iratok Magyarországról, 1933-1944* (The Wilhelmstrasse and Hungary. German Diplomatic Papers About Hungary, 1933-1944) (Budapest, 1968), p. 847 (hereafter, *A Wilhelmstrasse és Magyarország*). With the deterioration of the military situation in 1944, Heszlényi was placed at the head of the then newly formed Third Army. In connection with the Jewish question, he came into prominence again in September, 1944, when as commander of the Hungarian forces, which had occupied a part of southern Transylvania, including Arad, he issued a series of anti-Jewish edicts. A month later, he became one of the chief supporters of Ferenc Szálasi, leader of the Arrow Cross (*Nyilas Keresztes*) movement, in the coup that ousted Admiral Horthy. Professor Macartney claims that Heszlényi "killed himself on the frontier when the troops retreated into Austria." C. A. Macartney, *October Fifteenth: A History of Modern Hungary, 1929-1945* (Edinburgh, 1957), II, 340 (hereafter, Macartney). His name was listed in 1946, however, among Hungarian war criminals held by American authorities in Germany. See the letter of Major-General William S. Key to Lieutenant-General Sviridov, chairman of the Allied Control Commission in Hungary, June 12, 1946, in István Pintér and László Szabó, eds., *Criminals at Large* (Budapest, 1961), pp. 298-299.

7. Homlok was born in Késmárk, near Kosice (Kassa). He attended the Ludovika Military Academy and served on the General Staff. From 1927 to 1934, he served as military attaché in Paris. In 1934, he was reassigned to the General Staff, where he was for a while entrusted with the leadership of Section V, which dealt with the military-political implications of issues before the Staff. In this capacity, he played a leading role in 1938-1939, in the Hungarian drive against Carpatho-Ruthenia. In 1941, he was appointed military attaché in Berlin. In his dispatches, he warned about the imminence of the Russo-German war and insisted on the necessity of Hungary's military participation on the side of the Third Reich. Following the collapse of Germany Homlok fled to Austria, where he was "liberated" by the Americans. Shortly thereafter he was employed by the International Refugee Organization (IRO) of the United Nations in Austria and came to the United States in 1951. From 1952 to 1956, he worked for the Hungarian National Committee in New York. He retired in 1956, and died in New York in April, 1963. For further details on Homlok, consult the index pages of the following works: László Zsigmond, et al., eds. and comps., *Magyarország és a második világháború* (Hungary and the Second World War) (Budapest, 1961); *A Wilhelmstrasse és Magyarország*; Elek Karsai, *A budai Sándor palotában történt* (It Happened in the Sándor Palace of Buda) (Budapest, 1963); and Macartney.

8. Though this proposal was apparently kept alive until its implementation in the wake of the German occupation in 1944, neither Admiral Horthy nor Prime Minister Kállay made any reference to it in their memoirs. During an interview with the author on January 26, 1956, Kállay denied having even heard of Heszlényi.

9. See letter of Alfred Jodl, Chief of the OKW, to the German Foreign Office, July 21, 1942, in Randolph L. Braham, *The Destruction of Hungarian Jewry* (New York, 1963), Document 46 (hereafter RLB).

10. It is to Kállay's credit that even during 1942 he resisted the ever-pressing German demands for the deportation of the Jews. See RLB, Docs. No. 66-110.

11. Béla Vágó, "Germany and the Jewish Policy of the Kállay Government," *Hungarian-Jewish Studies*, II, p. 203. See also Doc. No. 488 in *A Wilhelmstrasse és Magyarország*, p. 661.

12. Kállay claims that before making the declaration relating to the planned expulsion of the Jews, he had a discussion "with the official leader of the Jews." Nicholas Kállay, *Hungarian Premier: A Personal Account of a Nation's Struggle in the Second World War* (New York, 1954), p. 99.

13. The roundup of the Jews of Slovakia began in March 1942. The first transport of 999 girls was taken to Auschwitz on March 26. By late May 1942, about 40,000 persons had been deported from the country. Livia Rothkirchen, *The Destruction of Slovak Jewry* (Jerusalem, 1961), pp. xxii-xxiii.

14. RLB, Doc. No. 46.

15. *Inland II, Geheim 58/1, 208/K213390. Auswärtiges Amt, Akten Betreffend Juden in Ungarn von August 1942 bis März 1948* (Politisches Archiv, Bonn) [hereafter *Inl.IIg*].

16. *Inl.IIg*. 208/K213391.

17. *Inl.IIg*. 208/K213388-389.

18. *Inl.IIg*. 208/K213385-386.

19. RLB, Doc. No. 47.

20. *Inl.IIg*. 208/K213381-382.

21. Roughly the total number of Jews in the territories acquired by Hungary during 1938-1941. See footnote 3.

22. Elek Karsai, *A budai vártól a gyepüig, 1941-1945* (From the Fort of Buda to the Borderland, 1941-1945) (Budapest, 1965), pp. 203-206.

23. Jenö Lévai, the noted expert on the Hungarian Jewish catastrophe, in a personal communication dated August 25, 1971, claims that the Fáy in question was Gedeon Fáy. His full name is Gedeon Fáy-Halász, and in fact he served in the Ministry of Foreign Affairs, when Prime Minister Kállay was its head. Fáy served in "the Minister's Cabinet" and his title was identified in the official register of the government as "*dr. min. s. titk.*" (*Dr. Minisztériumi segéd titkár*; Dr. Ministerial Assistant Secretary). *Magyarország tiszti cim- és névtára*, IL, 36. In 1943, he was promoted to head the Minister's cabinet. *Magyarország és a második világháború*, p. 498. In a letter to this author dated November 3, 1971, Dr. Aladár Szegedy-Maszák, the former head of the Political Section of the Hungarian Foreign Ministry (1943-1944), asserts that when he was attached to the Minister's Cabinet Fáy was "technically and administratively the personal secretary of Kállay in his capacity as Foreign Minister." According to Lévai (letter dated October 26, 1971), Fáy was transferred to the Political Section of the Foreign Ministry in March 1944. The Ministry was then headed by Prime Minister Sztójay, but was in fact under the direction of Dr. Mihály Jungerth-Arnóthy, the Deputy Foreign Minister. Gedeon Fáy-Halász went to the United States after the war, but moved to Munich in the late 1960s.

Nicholas Nagy-Talavera claims, and Raul Hilberg more humbly assumes, without providing any evidence, that the Fáy mentioned by Wisliceny was the notorious anti-Semite Baron László Vay, whose name Wisliceny may have misspelled. Nicholas Nagy-Talavera, *The Green Shirts and the Others. A History of Fascism in Hungary and Rumania* (Stanford, 1970), p. 184; Raul Hilberg, *The Destruction of the European Jews* (Chicago, 1961), pp. 522-523.

Baron László Vay also had an initiative of his own in connection with the solution of the Jewish problem in Hungary, but his German contact was, indirectly, Martin Bormann, *Reichsleiter* and chief of the Nazi Party chancellery.

A certain secretary of state named Fáy is also mentioned without any further identification by Lévai as having been a member of *Kaláka*, the secret society headed by László Baky, the notorious gendarmerie major and Hungarian Nazi leader who, as secretary of state in the Ministry of the Interior in the Sztójay government, was one of the few figures chiefly responsible for the destruction of Hungarian Jewry. This society continued to meet once a week even after Baky was removed from office on September 5, 1944, partially for his role in the attempted coup against Horthy on July 7-8. The information about *Kaláka* was provided by Baky himself in his testimony written in the Markó Street prison in Budapest in 1945. Jenö Lévai, *Fekete könyv a magyar zsidóság szenvedéseiröl* (Black Book on the Sufferings of Hungarian Jewry) (Budapest, 1946), p. 211.

The only other Fáy of any prominence in 1942 was István Fáy, secretary of state in the Ministry of Cults and Public Education. However, he is held by his contemporaries as totally unlikely to have initiated the resettlement proposal to Wisliceny. In his letter cited above, Szegedy-Maszák, for example, also declared that: "According to my own recollections and to some people familiar with the Hungarian scene, he [István Fáy] was not a Rightist in the Hungarian sense but a rather typical representative of the Bethlen establishment. While this does not exclude a certain degree of anti-Semitism, it does exclude extremism in every respect."

24. Dr. Gábor Szarka served as a section head in the Bratislava (Pozsony) mission of the Hungarian Foreign Trade Office. See *Magyarország tiszti cim- és névtára*, p. 323. According to Lévai (personal letter dated October 26, 1971), Szarka was transferred to Copenhagen in 1944.

25. Rothkirchen, *The Destruction of Slovak Jewry*, pp. xiv, xx.

26. *Ibid.*, p. xxv.

27. RLB, Doc. No. 74.

28. *Ibid.*

29. *Ibid.*, Doc. No. 48.

30. The request was forwarded on December 10, 1942, by Franz Sonnleithner, a member of the Foreign Minister's personal staff. *Ibid.*, Doc. No. 49.

31. *Ibid.*, Doc. No. 50.

32. This author at least was unsuccessful in locating the document in the archives of the German Foreign Office in Bonn.

33. *Magyarország tiszti cim- és névtára*, pp. 9, 13, 716.

34. In addition to Lukács and Vay, the delegation also included Professor Dezsö Laky, Pál Thuránszky, and Lajos Huszovszky, all members of the Lower House of Parliament. RLB, Doc. No. 96. A few weeks before the departure of the delegation, a group of Right-wing MÉP deputies handed Lukács a memorandum in which they called for, among other things, "a hard, militant, Right-wing policy, based on the Szeged Idea at home, with stern measures against subversive elements and new and effective measures against the Jews." Macartney, II, 209.

35. RLB, Doc. No. 96. Shortly after the German occupation, Vay was entrusted on April 5, 1944 by the caucus of the government party headed by Lukács to bring about the union of all the Rightist forces "willing to cooperate with the government party" in order to assure national unity. *A Wilhelmstrasse és Magyarország*, p. 814.

36. RLB, Docs. No. 97, 98.

37. *Ibid.*, Doc. No. 103.

38. Jenö Lévai, *Eichmann in Hungary* (Budapest, 1961), pp. 55-57.

39. RLB, Doc. No. 106.

40. *Ibid.*, Doc. No. 107.

41. György Ránki, *1944. március 19* (March 19, 1944) (Budapest, 1968), p. 30.

42. RLB, Doc. No. 110.

43. Miklós Szinai and László Szücs, eds., *The Confidential Papers of Admiral Horthy* (Budapest, 1965), pp. 267-269. Colonel Walter Warlimont, Alfred Jodl's deputy at OKW, intimates that the occupation was ordered because of "Hitler's rage and thirst for revenge against the Hungarian Regent" presumably over his demand of February 12. Walter Warlimont, *Inside Hitler's Headquarters, 1989-45* (New York, 1964), pp. 412-413.

44. In anticipation of a favorable conclusion of the conference, the Germans prepared a draft communiqué, which, however, was not signed. For the text of the communiqué, see *A Wilhelmstrasse és Magyarország*, pp. 782-783.

45. For the minutes of the Crown Council meeting, see *The Confidential Papers of Admiral Horthy*, pp. 278-290.

46. Albert Speer, *Inside the Third Reich* (New York, 1970), p. 395. Milch apparently acted in response to the decision that was taken in this respect by his superior, *Reichmarschall* Hermann Göring. Citing the concurrence of Hitler, Göring requested of Himmler, in a telegram dated February 14, 1944, that concentration-camp labor be provided for the building of underground aircraft factories. In his letter of March 9, 1944, Himmler assured Göring that plans for the allocation of about 100,000 inmates for this purpose were in the process of implementation. For the text of the correspondence between Göring and Himmler and their subordinates relating to this subject, see PS-1584 reproduced in International Military Tribunal, *Trial of the Major War Criminals Before the International Military Tribunal* (Nuremberg, 1947-1949), XXVII, 351-364.

47. *Ibid.*, p. 396.

48. *Ibid.*, p. 397.

49. Elek Karsai, A *budai vártól a gyepüig*, p. 689. See also Speer's summary (dated April 9, 1944) of his discussions with the *Führer* on April 6 and 7 relating to the employment of Jewish workers from Hungary, in Lévai, *Eichmann in Hungary*, p. 81.

50. Macartney, II, 280.

51. RLB, Doc. No. 133.

52. *Ibid.*, Doc. No. 134.

53. *Ibid.*, Doc. No. 135.

54. *Ibid.*, Docs. No. 139, 140.

55. *Ibid.*, Doc. No. 138. To the great sorrow of those who had hoped or believed that the Germans would not be able to obtain the railroad cars needed to effectuate the deportations in view of the great military pressures the Nazis were exposed to in 1944 both on the eastern and the western fronts, Eichmann managed to acquire the trains from the German military authorities because of the high priority the Nazis attached to the building of the underground aircraft factories which required Hungarian Jewish labor.

56. *Ibid.*, Doc. No. 141.

57. An account of the "ghettoization" and deportation process is beyond the scope of this paper.

58. See excerpts from the minutes of the meeting of the Council of Ministers of April 26, 1944, in Lévai, *Eichmann in Hungary*, p. 82.

59. RLB, Doc. No. 150. It is worth remembering that these first transports were put together not by Eichmann's *Sonderkommando* but by the *Honvédség.*

60. Perhaps Horthy had in mind only the shipment of labor battalion draftees or only of able-bodied "Galician" Jews from the territories acquired between 1938 and 1941. He alludes to the former in his highly slanted memoirs. See Horthy, *Memoirs* (New York, 1957), p. 219.

61. This was revealed during the trial of Veesenmayer. See the transcript of the Ministries Trial (Court IV, Case 11), testimony of July 22, 1948, p. 13243.

62. Testimony by Winkelmann involving Veesenmayer, October 18, 1948, *ibid.*, pp. 26172-26173.

63. Macartney, II, 238-239. See also Ernst Kienast's statement of August 14, 1947, *Documents on the German Government prepared by the Allies to be used at Nuremberg* (hereafter NG), 2528.)

64. Veesenmayer's testimony on July 22, 1948, transcript version of Ministries Trial, p. 13260.

65. Lévai, *Fekete könyv a magyar zsidóság szenvedéseiröl*, p. 128.

66. *Ibid.*

67. Ránki, *1944. március 19*, p. 175.

68. Macartney, II, 283.

69. Perényi himself was informed by Samu Káhán-Frankl and Imre Reiner of the Jewish Council. Ernö Munkácsi, *Hogyan történt?* (How did it happen?) (Budapest, 1947), p. 142.

70. *Ibid.*

71. Macartney, II, 283.

72. Lévai, *Eichmann in Hungary*, p. 119. This telegram by Sztójay, sent out in his capacity as Prime Minister, is an official document proving that the Hungarian government he headed permitted the deportation of Jews on the basis of an agreement with the Germans. See also Lévai's evaluation of this document in his *Fehér könyv. Külföldi akciók zsidók megmentésére* (White Book. Foreign Actions for the Rescuing of the Jews) (Budapest, 1946), pp. 54-55.

73. Macartney, II, 280.

74. The *Einsatzgruppe* was composed of only 500 to 600 *Gestapo* and SD members who operated under the immediate command of *SS-Standartenführer* Hans Geschke, the *BdS* (*Befehlshaber der Sicherheitspolizei*; Commander of the Security Police) in Hungary. Eichmann's *Sonderkommando* had only 200 to 300 men available for the Final Solution. Macartney, II, 228.

75. Among these schemes one can cite the techniques employed by the Nazis to reassure the leaders of Hungarian Jewry about the "safety" of their community; the mailing of "arrived safely" cards by the first deportees to "Waldsee" (Auschwitz) written just before they were sent into the gas chambers; the offer to sell lives for trucks and other goods (the Kasztner-Brand mission); and the saving of a handful of Jews as evidence of goodwill (the Kasztner deal).

76. RLB, Doc. No. 147.

77. *Ibid.*, Doc. No. 149.

78. *Ibid.*, Doc. No. 158.

79. Höss' affidavit (3868-PS) in *Nazi Conspiracy and Aggression* (Washington, D.C., 1946), VI, 787.

80. Currently available evidence clearly indicates that the leadership of Hungarian Jewry as well as some of the leading members of the government were aware of the realities of Auschwitz. Testifying at the Veesenmayer trial on March 19, 1948, Kasztner declared: "We had, as early as 1942, a complete picture of what had been happening in the east with the Jews deported to Auschwitz and the other concentration camps." Transcript version of the Ministries Trial, p. 3622. On August 2, 1944, when the government discussed the possible resumption of the deportations, the Minister of Defense, Lajos Csatay, who later committed suicide, declared sarcastically that he would be in favor of the deportations if the "German Minister gave a written assurance that the displaced Jews would not be burnt at Auschwitz." Lévai, *Eichmann in Hungary*, pp. 10, 11, 137.

81. This is merely the official figure given by Veesenmayer concerning the deportations from May 15 through July 9, 1944. RLB, Docs. No. 174, 182, 193. Before Hungary was finally liberated on April 4, 1945, an additional 100,000 Jews fell victim to the Nazi terror. Added to the over 60,000 Jews who were killed in the labor battalions or during the Kamenets Podolsk and Novi Sad massacres, the casualties incurred during the Nazi period bring the total number of victims of the Hungarian Jewish catastrophe to over 600,000.*

82. While it is true that the master plan had been successfully implemented primarily because of the Germans' organizational and directional efficiency and the Hungarians' contribution of the *gendarmerie*, the police, and the entire state apparatus, its success was also advanced, if not assured, *inter alia*, by: (1) The failure of Horthy to resign upon his return from Klessheim on March 19, 1944, thereby assuring the legitimacy of both the German occupation and the Sztójay government; (2) The absence of any meaningful Hungarian opposition or resistance; (3) The passivity of the rest of the world, including the Allies; and (4) The shortsightedness if not outright though unwitting cooperation of the Jewish leadership, including the establishment-oriented Jewish Council and the Zionist leaders. Important as these factors are, they are beyond the immediate scope of this study.

83. Eugene (Jenö) Lévai, *Black Book on the Martyrdom of Hungarian Jewry* (Zurich, 1948), p. 139.

84. Jenö Lévai, *Zsidósors Magyarországon* (Jewish Fate in Hungary) (Budapest, 1948), p. 101.

---

* According to investigations made in the early 1990s, the losses of Hungarian Jewry were reduced to around 550,000. See Randolph L. Braham, *The Politics of Genocide: The Holocaust in Hungary* (New York: Columbia University press, 1994), pp. 1296-99.

5

The Official Jewish Leadership of Wartime Hungary

As a political scientist fascinated by historical studies in general, and by those of the Holocaust in particular, I am—as are all my colleagues at this symposium—keenly aware of the responsibility we share as chroniclers and scholars. I am fully cognizant of the fact that as historians we must, before making assessments, however tentative and qualified these may be, study and analyze the attitude and behavior of the historical figures—in this case those of the Jewish Council leaders—in the context of the time and place in which they played their parts. I am also aware that we must attempt to reconstruct the historical situation in which these leaders operated as faithfully and as exactly as available sources will permit.

Having identified but some of the premises which scholars often take for granted, I must hasten to state that history and historians have not been kind to the leaders of Hungarian Jewry—and perhaps justifiably so. The thrust of their accusations was generally against Hungarian Jewish leaders who failed to:

- Provide meaningful assistance to their oppressed and persecuted brethren in the neighboring Nazi-dominated countries;
- Accurately inform the Jewish masses of Hungary of the realities of the Nazi persecutions and concentration-extermination camp system, even though they were aware of the program for the implementation of the Final Solution;
- Take adequate precautionary measures for their own safety for, unlike the leaders of other Jewish communities of Europe, they had

Reprinted from *Patterns of Jewish Leadership in Nazi Europe, 1939-1945*, Yisrael Gutman and Cynthia J. Haft, eds. (Jerusalem: Yad Vashem, 1979), with permission of the publisher.

almost five years to prepare for the possible ultimate catastrophe; and

— Organize any collective resistance, or provide the kind of courageous leadership after the German occupation that the extraordinarily perilous conditions required.

This paper aims at exploring the validity of these accusations by:

— Evaluating the functional-operational characteristics of the official wartime Hungarian Jewish leadership;

— Analyzing the quality and effectiveness of the leadership under conditions of stress; and

— Providing a typology of leadership in the context of Hungarian-Jewish communal political life.

The most charitable historians and chroniclers of the Holocaust, and especially those deeply concerned with the extremely sensitive issues relating to the activities of the Jewish Councils and the resistance movements, decided, for linguistic and many other reasons, not to deal with Hungary. This is the case, for example, in Isaiah Trunk's monumental and valuable *Judenrat*,[1] and Reuben Ainsztein's book: *Jewish Resistance in Nazi Occupied Eastern Europe*.[2] Their indices contain no references to Hungary, nor to any of the leaders of the Hungarian Jewish Council.

In his introduction, though, Ainsztein is rather caustic about the stance of the Hungarian Jews, wondering how a community that produced "such men of action as Béla Kun and Mátyás Rákosi could not produce better leaders than it did in its greatest hour of need...." He is just as harsh and self-assured in placing the blame for the failure to resist on the part of the Hungarian Jewish community. He states:

> ...to many Hungarian Jews who have survived, the responsibility for their failure as a community to fight back against the combined power of the Nazi machinery of genocide and Hungarian anti-Semitism is in no doubt. They place it squarely on the shoulders of their self-appointed leaders who formed the Jewish Council, and, in particular, on those of its chairman, Dr. Israel Kastner.*

* Dr. Kasztner was actually one of the leaders of *Va'ad ha-Hazzalah* and not on the Council.

This is as unequivocal an indictment of wartime Hungarian Jewish leadership as can be found in postwar general and Jewish historiography.

Putting aside Ainsztein's obviously erroneous observation as to the self-appointment of the Council and its alleged leadership by Kasztner, many questions still remain open as to the caliber, character, and quality of Hungarian Jewish leadership during the Second World War. A complete response to these questions requires not only an understanding of the background and *modus operandi* of the various Jewish leaders, but also an intimate familiarity with the systemic components of the semi-Fascist Horthy regime, including its political culture, governmental structure, and socio-economic policies, which are clearly beyond the scope of this paper.[3]

Any discussion of leadership—and in this context we may define leadership as "the exercise of uncommon influence upon the followers of a particular community"—must begin with an evaluation of the power upon which it relies and on its operational characteristics. This premise is equally valid with respect to the assessment of a denominational leadership and to the evaluation of a national political elite.

It is a truism to state that the Hungarian Jewish leaders—both central and local—did not have the power to make independent decisions. Before the German occupation of Hungary on March 19, 1944, they, as the leaders of all other officially recognized denominations, had a degree of authority over the communities which they administered. The nature and limits of this authority were stipulated by the Hungarian Royal Ministry of Cults and Public Education (*Magyar királyi Vallás- és Közoktatásügyi Minisztérium*),[4] and were exercised under its control. After the occupation, the Jewish leaders were forced to operate first under the exclusive authority of the SS, and after a short while under the SS and the German-supported Hungarian government. Within the latter, control over the Jews was transferred from the Ministry of Cults and Public Education to the newly-established Jewish Section of the Ministry of the Interior (*Belügyminisztérium*) which was dominated by László Baky and László Endre, the two Secretaries of State who are universally recognized as among those primarily responsible for the destruction of Hungarian Jewry.

It is also a truism that in Hungary, as in Nazi-dominated Europe in general, the Jewish leaders could not possibly have played a decisive role in determining the tempo, or the ultimate outcome, of the Nazi's Final Solution program. Consequently, ultimate responsibility for the destruction of Hungarian Jewry must be placed squarely and almost exclusively on the German and Hungarian authorities who exercised total power through their monopolistic control over the instruments of coercion, including the mass media, police, gendarmerie, and civil service. At this point, it may be superfluous to state that in contrast to the pre-occupation period, the traditional Hungarian Jewish leaders, acting as members of the Judenrat, exercised quite a bit of power. In fact, in one of their first appeals addressed to Hungarian Jewry, they reminded the community that they "had been given responsibility, as well as absolute power, to exercise control over spiritual and material needs, as well as the authority to exploit Jewish labor."[5]

In light of multiple postwar accusations, the question of whether the Holocaust could have been avoided, or its impact mitigated, cannot be answered adequately without an objective evaluation of the quality and effectiveness of wartime Hungarian Jewish leadership. For unlike the leaders of most other European Jewish communities, the national leaders of Hungarian Jewry were fully aware of the realities of the Nazis' Final Solution program by the time the mass concentration and deportation program was launched in Hungary in May 1944, if not much earlier.

One must agree with Professor Jacob Katz when he states that the Holocaust has to be conceived as an absolute *novum*, something new and unexpected, even by those well acquainted with the past history of Jewish suffering.[6] But are these perspicacious observations really applicable to the national leaders of Hungarian Jewry? The reactions of the Jewish Council of Budapest, unlike those of the Judenräte elsewhere, must be measured on a somewhat different scale. What was *unknown and unimaginable* to other Councils, was fully *known* and quite *imaginable* to the national Jewish leaders of Hungary. They were, according to the evidence available to us, the only ones who had *prima facie* evidence of the Nazis' extermination program *before* the mass deportations began.[7]

Moreover, the Jews of Hungary, while suffering the iniquities imposed by several major anti-Jewish laws, and mourning the loss of thousands who died in the labor service system,[8] and at Kamenets-Podolsk and Ujvidék[9] (the two major massacres perpetrated before the German occupation), fared relatively well, at least for the first four and a half years of the war. During this long period of uneasy tranquility, the Jewish leaders, although they themselves witnessed the inferno engulfing Nazi-dominated Europe, failed to keep the governmental and political leaders, as well as the Jewish masses, fully informed, nor did they implement any of the meaningful precautionary measures suggested by the many Jewish refugees from the neighboring countries.

Indeed, although the Jewish masses lived almost in the immediate vicinity of Auschwitz, they, as almost all other Hungarians, had no idea of the gas chambers and of the mass murders perpetrated in the German death camps. They, as their leaders, deluded themselves into believing that at any rate, what happened in Poland and elsewhere could not possibly happen in Hungary, where the destiny of the Jews had been intertwined with that of the Hungarian Christians for over a thousand years. The well-informed Jewish leaders failed to keep the Jewish masses abreast of what was transpiring in the neighboring countries and, good law-abiding citizens that they were, they heeded all the strict censorship regulations, and prohibited the use of synagogues for such "propaganda" purposes.

The causes behind the lack of adequate preparation for the possibility of a catastrophe befalling Hungarian Jews were many and variegated. Two major reasons were the long-standing inability of the various communities to transcend their traditional, and ostensibly irreconcilable, differences, and effect transcongregational unity; and the failure to adhere to the democratic process in the organization and administration of the Jewish communities in general, and of their central institutions in particular.

The sudden occupation of Hungary by the Germans found the Jewish community as conflict-ridden and disunited as it had been since 1868, when it had tried for the first and last time to overcome its political and religious differences. Even after the "White Terror" (1919-1920)[10], when some of the illusions of the former "Golden Era" (1867-1914)[11] were dissipated, few, if any, attempts were made to end the constant bickering within and among the three major official and semi-official communities—the Neolog,[12] the Orthodox,[13] and the *Status Quo*[14]—as well as the interminable quarrels with the quasi-illegal and basically ineffective Zionist Organization.[15] Aside from the bickering among the three established communities over the content and form of religious practices, Hungarian Jewry was also plagued by political conflicts between the assimilated-acculturated group and the Zionists; by the conflicting economic concerns of the rich and the poor; and by the rivalries among the larger and semi-autonomous congregations,[16] compounded by the jealousy and personal animosity motivating many of the leaders of these communities in the pursuit of their narrow parochial aims.

In terms of the typology of leadership developed by Carl J. Friedrich, the Hungarian Jewish leaders who dominated communal life were of the "maintaining" and "protecting" rather than the "initiating" type. They rarely, if ever, initiated any line of action that transcended the established system of values. Firmly committed to the values and principles of the traditional conservative-aristocratic system, and convinced that the Jewish interests were intimately intertwined with those of the Magyars, they never contemplated the use of independent political techniques for the advancement of Jewish interests *per se*. They proudly considered themselves "Magyars of the Jewish faith" (*zsidóvallású magyarok*). Composed of rich, patriotic, and generally conservative elements, this leadership aimed at contributing to the maintenance of the established order by faithfully obeying the governmental directives and by fully associating itself with the values, beliefs, and interests of Hungarian society in general. At the same time, this leadership did everything in its power to protect the basic interests of the community, from which in return it expected not only acclaim, but, above all, voluntary subservience. Its authority was legitimate in terms of two of Max Weber's three major criteria: it enjoyed the sanctity of tradition, however brief and undemocratic in historical terms, and profited from the aura of legality provided by governmental and communal authorization. It was completely non-charismatic; none of the leaders was possessed of any exceptional personal qualities. While devoted to the welfare and continuing progress of the Jewish community, the leaders of Hungarian Jewry were neither inspirational nor highly intellectual.

The central as well as the local communal organizations and institutions were, to a large extent, established and operated in an undemocratic fashion. Franchise was limited by property and other qualifications, with the practical result that the leadership was drawn almost exclusively from the wealthiest strata of the community and only a few professionals played an active role in the general intellectual and political life of the locality. Moreover, in Trianon Hungary proper, the leadership of the *kehillot* tended to comprise primarily the Hungarian patriotic, anti-Zionist, assimiliationist elements. Because of their prominence in the communities, these leaders were routinely renominated and reelected; but while most of them rendered great service to the masses, there was very limited organic contact between them.

Most of the Neolog and Orthodox leaders of the central organizations and institutions of Hungarian Jewry in Budapest belonged to the upper middle class, and some to the lower nobility.[17] Reflecting their class background and status, they were basically conservative, and tended to identify with the political and socio-economic views, as well as the irredentist-nationalist aspirations, of their Hungarian Christian counterparts. Conspicuously absent from this group were the totally assimilated Jewish industrial magnates. The group also failed to attract, or refused to admit, any leading artists, intellectuals, Zionist figures, women, or young people.

Although they were guided by high moral standards as well as by the desire to advance the religious and social welfare of the Jewish community, the *modus operandi* of these national leaders tended to be highly formal and legalistic, in emulation of the behavior of their gentry counterparts. Unlike many of the Polish and Romanian national Jewish leaders, for example, they shunned using the political arena for the protection and advancement of Jewish interests *per se*, opposing with equal vehemence both the Zionists and the proponents of a Hungarian Jewish Party. Consequently, their response to the ever exacerbating anti-Jewish measures during the interwar period was apologetic in nature and isolated from the general struggle of European Jewry. Their loyalty to the Hungarian nation, as shown *inter alia* by their vigorous irredentist struggle for the rectification of the "injustices of Trianon," and their attachment to the gentry-aristocratic establishment, remained unshaken. Perhaps considering the great strides Hungarian Jewry had made during the "Golden Era" of liberalism, these leaders strove to safeguard those rights which the Jews still enjoyed in the wake of the major anti-Jewish laws; and to restore, if possible, the *Interessengemeinschaft* that characterized the prewar period. They tended to pursue these objectives, however, without abandoning the traditional operational techniques that were proving increasingly ineffective, if not clearly counter-productive. Having no experience in militant political struggles for exclusively Jewish causes, lacking direct contact with the masses of Hungarian Jewry whose intimate problems and spiritual world they did not adequately represent or understand, and voluntarily isolated from the concerns of world Jewry, these leaders emerged during the German occupation as singularly inept at providing the kind of leadership demanded by these extraordinarily perilous times.[18]

The weaknesses and strengths, trials and tribulations, perceptions and rationalizations of the traditional leaders of Hungarian Jewry in the Jewish Council[19] can be illustrated by the position and attitude of Samu Stern, the then seventy-year old President of the Council. At the time of the occupation, he was the President of both the Central Bureau of the Jews of Hungary and of the Jewish Community of Pest (*Pesti Izraelita Hitközség*), the country's largest and most influential congregation. A Counselor of the Hungarian Royal Court (*Magyar királyi udvari tanácsos*), Stern was a very successful businessman enjoying an excellent relationship with the aristocratic-conservative elements of Hungarian society. Within the Jewish community, he was one of the most highly respected and well-liked leaders.

Stern's generosity, combined with his ability to collect large amounts of money for Jewish causes, earned him universal esteem. He was the principal representative of, and one of the chief spokesmen for the Neolog, the assimiliationist, and anti-Zionist stratum of Hungarian Jewry. Yet he remained conscious of his deep Jewish roots, and did everything *legally* possible to advance the cause and interests of the Jews of Hungary as he understood them. His tragedy and that of the Jewish Council resided at least partially in the fact that the aristocratic-conservative Christian leadership of Hungary, with which he had a very positive relationship, was itself partly dispersed. With the arrest of the leading members of this class during the first days following the occupation, the Jewish community became totally isolated and an easy prey for the SS. The tragedy was compounded by the official Jewish leaders' insistence upon relying on traditional legal methods, such as the filing of appeals and petitions—methods which had proved highly effective during the pre-occupation semi-parliamentary era, but were totally inadequate for the extraordinarily perilous period of Nazi rule.[20] Yet in many ways Stern showed great personal courage in dealing with the *Moloch*, and did everything possible to win that which was, to his mind, decisive—the race with time.[21]

In discussing his ascendance to the presidency of the Jewish Council, Stern claims that the Germans had not duped him and that he was aware of what they had done throughout occupied Europe. He also states:

> ...I had heard enough about the methods of the Gestapo's ill-reputed Jewish Department [Eichmann's section in the Reich Security Main Office] to know that they always shunned sensation, disliked creating panic and fear, worked noiselessly, coolly and in the deepest secrecy, so that the listless, ignorant victims might go without an inkling of what awaited them even while the wagon was traveling with them towards death.... I knew their habits, deeds, and terrifying reputation....

He further asserts that the other members of the Council knew as much as he did when they consented to serve.[22]

Nevertheless, Stern accepted the role of leader of the Jewish Council, which technically had no legal basis since it was established under the orders of, and at the beginning at least was responsible exclusively to, the SS. He explains his decision as follows:

> ... A prisoner at the mercy of his jailer is not in a position to object to the cell into which he is thrown.... I had spent sixteen years at the head of the Jewish Community of Pest.... In my eyes it would have been cowardly, an unmanly and unjustifiably selfish flight on my part to let down my brethren in the faith during the very instant when they were in dire need of being led, when men having both experience and connections, ready to make sacrifices, might prove useful to a certain extent. What would Jewry abroad have thought of me if I had looked for some issue to escape doing my duty?...I was aware that a race with time was on. It was anticipated that the war would end within months in a complete defeat of Germany. I calculated though, that even these

> few months might prove too long a time for flight, that meanwhile other help might be required. I thought also of the possibility of claiming Governor Horthy's help for rescuing the Jews; that man whom I knew for two decades, whom I had assaulted with demands in Jewish affairs any time it had been necessary. I knew, as I had to, that in our state of utter helplessness only the Governor could be of help within the country, and no help could be forthcoming from the outside....[23] I...kept concentrating all my thoughts on the stringent necessity to delay, with the help of tactical moves, that supreme danger—the annihilation of Hungarian Jewry in its entirety. For an aged man as I was, with health already undermined by time, it would certainly have been an easier alternative to step aside and not take that onerous role of the Council upon my shoulders. But would not just stepping aside have been unscrupulous?...It is not good for the flock to trade an experienced shepherd for an inexperienced one who just happened to be accepted in the midst of tempest.[24]

Stern soon proved to be unable to cope successfully with the grave problems which confronted the community. It should be pointed out, though, that most of them were beyond his control, and would surely have stymied men of much greater intellectual and leadership qualities. Stern's contacts with the Regent and the other strata of the traditional conservative-aristocratic leadership in Hungarian society were severed; the resources of the community had been almost totally exhausted within a short time; the new Hungarian authorities had completely abandoned their citizens of the Jewish faith who had so loyally served the nation in the past; the Nazis and their Hungarian hirelings were pressing on relentlessly with their Final Solution program. However, Stern still attempted everything in his power under the circumstances and given his own background, tradition, and experience, to save whatever he could until the arrival of the Soviet troops which was generally, if somewhat over-optimistically, considered imminent.

The central Jewish Council had been conceived as a "representative" body, a kind of "unity" or "coalition" council. It included a number of members with whom the dominant Neolog leaders had not had intimate contact in the past, and after its reorganization late in April 1944, one member whom they regarded with great suspicion and distrust.[25] For this reason, Stern and his two intimate Neolog friends—Ernö Pető and Károly Wilhelm—acted as a triumvirate.[26]

The Council held formal meetings only rarely; on the other hand, the three had frequent discussions, to which they occasionally invited many of the administrative officials of the Council.

The close cooperation among the three Neolog assimilationist traditional leaders of Hungarian Jewry, throughout their tenure on the Council, was based as much on mutual trust and long-standing personal friendship as it was on their collective distrust of some of the other Council members. It was strengthened by the dictates of the frequent emergencies which required speedy decisions that would have been more difficult for a larger deliberative body.

The secrecy of the three, however, was maintained to the chagrin of several of their colleagues on the Council who not only mistrusted their judgment, but also resented the fact that the other Council members had to share responsibility for decisions which they had no part in making. The most prominent of these "rebels" were Béla Berend and Lajos Stöckler. They tended to oppose the triumvirate on political, social, and religious grounds. Berend and Stöckler claim to have attempted to represent and defend the interests of the "small," "unprotected" Jews, such as the ones in the so-called Star Houses and in the Budapest ghetto, who did not share the "privileges" granted to exempted and converted Jews. They tended to look upon the members of the triumvirate as the elitist representatives, the propertied "upper classes."[27]

One of the primary functions that the SS envisioned for the Jewish Council was to lull the large Jewish masses into submission by providing them with a false sense of security. The Nazis were, of course, interested in avoiding an uprising on the style of the Warsaw ghetto, and shrewdly manoeuvered the Council into actions calculated to assure a calm atmosphere in the Jewish communities.[28] The Jews, individually and collectively, were frequently warned that only strict compliance with all the rules and regulations of the German and Hungarian Nazi authorities would "guarantee [their] civilian life within the permitted framework." The Council emphasized that Jews who fulfilled all their responsibilities would enjoy "the same treatment, food, and pay as the other workers," and would be protected. A similar stand was also adopted by members of the Rabbinate. Dr. Ferenc Havesi, the Neolog Chief Rabbi, urged the Jews to "pray to God for yourself, your family, your children, but primarily and above all, for your Hungarian homeland! Love of homeland, fulfillment of duty, and prayer should be your guiding light!"[29] In his appeal of April 20, 1944, Dr. Ernö Boda, a Judenrat member, reminded the Jews that they were not only the People of the Book, but also that of the Law, and therefore "must abide by all, even the most severe measures, without any deliberation or pondering." The Council continued to call upon the Jews to "trust and believe," and show "unconditional understanding confidence," even after the deportations began on May 15, with the transport of approximately twelve thousand Jews per day.[30]

Unlike the Jewish Councils in many other parts of Nazi-occupied Europe, the central and local Councils of Hungary were never confronted with the agony of selecting Jews for deportation and eventual extermination. This function was fulfilled speedily and effectively by the SS and their Hungarian hirelings. The Council's involuntary actions, however, largely contributed to the smoothness with which the ghettoization and deportations were implemented. The desire to assure law and order was also one of the primary motives of the SS in their dealings with the Zionist leaders associated with the *Va'ad ha-Hazzalah* (Rescue Committee) of Budapest, with whom they had deceptively engaged in special "rescue" deals.[31] Although these leaders were, at least subconsciously, increasingly aware of the function that was assigned to them, they were also helplessly ensnared. Power was in the hands of the Germans, who also enjoyed the enthusiastic support of the anti-Semitic elements of Hungary which placed the country's instruments of coercion at the Nazis' disposal. The Hungarians, unlike the Danes and the Western Europeans in general, were basically passive in attitude and many of them, intoxicated by the vicious anti-Semitic propaganda of the previous two decades, were eager to share in the wealth expropriated from the Jews. Under these conditions, the leaders of the Jewish Council tried to save whatever they could through dilatory tactics, and later by reestablishing contact with Admiral Horthy and some of the other traditional Hungarian figures. The Zionist leaders for their part followed the so-called "SS-line," within the framework of the "Europa Plan" launched in Bratislava in a vain attempt to buy off the Germans.[32] Both approaches were equally futile from the point of view of the provincial Jews who, with the exception of some twenty thousand, were deported to Auschwitz within a very brief span.

The ineffectiveness of the Jewish leadership was, to some extent, also influenced by the leaders' distorted perception of the Nazis' objectives in Hungary. For quite a while they deluded themselves into believing that the Germans would not apply the same draconic measures to solve the Jewish question in Hungary as they did elsewhere, based on:

— The promises and declarations made by the SS officers during their first meetings with the Jewish leaders;

— The fact that the Regent, who had earlier concurred with Kállay's Jewish policy, was left at the helm;

— The realization that the military situation of the Germans at the time of the occupation of Hungary was much worse than during the period of the "Solution to the Jewish Question" elsewhere in Europe;

— The expectation that the Germans, aware of the unpopular character of the occupation, would want to pacify, rather than antagonize, the population;

— The fact that, despite the plethora of anti-Jewish laws, the situation of the Jews in Hungary was better than it was elsewhere;

— The expectation that proposals for a radical solution in Hungary would bring forth vocal political opposition in Parliament, as had been demonstrated during the adoption of the anti-Jewish laws in 1938-1942; and

— The realization that the Red Army was already at the Carpathians.[33]

The distorted viewpoint of the Jewish leaders was reinforced by the personal favors accorded to them, as well as their families, by the SS. This was actually a standard SS approach in all the Nazi-occupied countries, not only towards Jewish leaders, but also towards local officials, to acquire their confidence and ensure their cooperation. In the case of the Jews, these favors consisted primarily of the exemption of the leaders and their immediate families from many of the anti-

Jewish measures.[34] However, these favors were usually ephemeral, for at the close of the ghettoization and deportation program in a particular area, the leaders themselves were usually also rounded up and subjected to the same treatment the others had incurred. This was obviously what the Nazis planned for Hungary as well, and in fact the scheme was implemented in the provinces, but Horthy's decision to put an end to the deportations on July 7, 1944 saved the leaders of the Central Council, as well as the other Jews of Budapest, from sharing the fate of their counterparts in most of the provincial ghettos.

The most surprising element with regard to the Nazi policy in Hungary is that the Hungarian Jewish leaders, although quite well-informed as to Nazi techniques, failed to act any differently from their counterparts elsewhere who did not have the benefit of this knowledge. For whatever reasons, it remains a historical fact that the wartime leaders of Hungarian Jewry, helpless and deprived of their traditional contacts, unwittingly and unwillingly did cooperate with the aggressors in the implementation of at least some preliminary aspects of the anti-Jewish drive, constantly rationalizing their actions as advantageous to the community under the given conditions.

Because of their limited forces and eagerness to avoid unnecessarily antagonizing the local population in Hungary as elsewhere in the German sphere of influence, the Nazis utilized the Jews and local authorities in implementing many of the anti-Jewish measures. Although the Jewish leaders were motivated by the desire to maintain positive relations with the Germans, who at first had exclusive power over the Jews, and to gain time in order to save Jewish lives, they were the ones who, *inter alia*, lulled the masses into a false sense of security. They issued many of the internment summonses; requisitioned apartments; distributed the yellow badges; effectuated the sequestration of the Jews in special buildings; and surrendered large sums of money. Against their will and their intentions, they became the helpless instruments with which the Nazis implemented many of their sinister designs.[35]

Could the Jewish leaders have acted differently? What would have happened had they resigned from the Council? Just as Horthy thought on his return from Schloss Klessheim, the traditional legitimist leaders of Jewry calculated that, by staying at the helm instead of escaping or resigning in a cowardly fashion, they could at least mitigate, if not totally avoid, their losses. Had they resigned *en masse* there is no doubt that the Nazis and their Hungarian hirelings would easily have found another, or even a third, set of Jewish leaders to replace them. Had they not implemented the orders relating to internments and the requisitioning of apartments, chances are good that the German and Hungarian units would have found a way to carry out these internments and requisitions more cruelly.

On the other hand, while the resignation of Stern and his colleagues would certainly have incurred their immediate arrest and possible execution, the Jewish masses might thus have learned of the realities of the German occupation early. Also, they would perhaps not have followed the instructions of nonentities and Jewish quislings as obediently as they did those of the traditional leaders whom they trusted. It was exactly for this reason that the Germans insisted on retaining the old, traditional, and trusted leaders of the Jewish communities on the Jewish Councils.

Conversely, it is safe to assume that had Stern and his associates refused to undertake the tasks assigned to them by the Germans, and by some miracle still survived the ordeal while hundreds of thousands of Jews were massacred, they would certainly have been condemned by other survivors for having held positions of power only while there was prestige and honor associated with them, and for having abandoned the community in its darkest hour, as some of the central and local leaders—including Zionists—had done. In spite of the obvious risks involved, the leaders of the Council decided to accept their onerous burden in the hope of mitigating, if not averting, the catastrophe looming over Hungarian Jewry. They had hoped to achieve this by dilatory tactics calculated to win "the race with time." As others almost everywhere else in Nazi-dominated Europe, they appear to have tried to come to terms with the oppressors in order to try to stymie their sinister objectives, and to save as many Jewish lives as possible under the extraordinarily perilous circumstances.

They were indeed shortsighted in their naïve optimism; they were obviously remiss in failing to prepare for a possible catastrophe; they were certainly devoid of any meaningful national Jewish consciousness; they were almost oblivious to the suffering of Jews elsewhere in Nazi-dominated Europe;[36] and they were woefully inadequate in their leadership after the occupation. The currently available evidence, however, does not lend itself to the conclusion that the Jewish Council, as a whole, acted in willful violation of the best interests of Hungarian Jewry under the extraordinary conditions of Nazi rule.

NOTES

1. I. Trunk, *Judenrat, The Jewish Councils in Eastern Europe Under Nazi Occupation*, New York, 1972.

2. R. Ainsztein, *Jewish Resistance in Nazi-Dominated Eastern Europe*, New York, 1974.

3. Some of these elements are discussed by E. Mendelsohn in his "The East European Jewish Community and its Leadership During the Interwar Period," pp. 1-12 in this volume.

4. Within the Ministry, the denominations were under the direct jurisdiction of the Main Section for Cults (*Vallásügyi föcsoport*). In the case of the Jews, the Main Section for Cults exercised direct control over the Central Bureau of the Jews of Hungary (*Magyarországi Izraeliták Országos Irodája*), the umbrella organization of Hungarian Jewry, the eight major communal districts (*községkerületek*), the Central Bureau of the Autonomous Orthodox Jewish Community of Hungary (*Magyarországi Autonom Orthodox Izraelita Hitfelekezet Központi Irodája*), and over the two major educational institutions of the community: the Ferenc József National Theological Institute (*A Ferenc József Országos Rabbiképzö Intézet*), and the National Jewish Teacher Training Institute (*Az Országos Izraelita Tanitóképzö Intézet*). The eight communal districts did not include the Jewish communities in the territories of *Felvidék* (Upper Province) and Kárpátalja (Carpatho-Ruthenia) which were reacquired from Czechoslovakia in 1938-39, Northern Transylvania which was reacquired from Romania in 1940, and Délvidék (the Bačka and adjacent areas) which was reacquired from Yugoslavia in 1941. These were still in the process of administrative reorganization. *Magyarországi tiszti cim- és névtára* ("Title and Name Register of Hungary"), Budapest, 1942, p. 559.

5. R. L. Braham, "The Role of the Jewish Council in Hungary: A Tentative Assessment," *Yad Vashem Studies*, Vol. X, Jerusalem, 1974, p. 96.

6. J. Katz, "Was the Holocaust Predictable?" *Commentary*, May 1975, pp. 41-48.

7. R. L. Braham, "What Did They Know and When?" *The Politics of Genocide: The Destruction of the Jews of Hungary*. [See study 2 in this volume.]

8. For details, consult R. L. Braham, *The Hungarian Labor Service System, 1939-1945*, Boulder, 1977.

9. R. L. Braham, "The Kamenets-Podolsk and Délvidék Massacres: Prelude to the Holocaust in Hungary," *Yad Vashem Studies*, Vol. IX, Jerusalem, 1973, pp. 133-156.

10. The terror of the counter-revolutionary murder squads which followed the overthrow of Béla Kun's dictatorship of the proletariat of March-August 1919, claimed thousands of lives, including many Jews. For details see D. Sulyok, *A magyar tragédia* ("The Hungarian Tragedy"), Newark, 1954, pp. 257-276.

11. The "Golden Era" of Hungarian Jewry is generally identified as the period extending from its emancipation in 1867-68 until World War I. During this period the Jews made great strides in industry, commerce, and the liberal professions.

12. The Neolog community comprised the assimiliationist strata of Hungarian Jewry, which tended to deviate from traditional Orthodox practices of Judaism; for

example, they used choirs and organ music in the synagogues, permitted decorations in cemeteries, and emphasized some of the ethical and esthetic aspects in religious instruction. The Neologs were predominant in the central leadership, as well as in that of most communities of Trianon Hungary.

13. The Orthodox section of Hungarian Jewry was the faction that insisted on strict adherence to traditional values and practices in Judaism.

14. The *Status quo* or *Status quo-ante* section of Hungarian Jewry comprised the communities that refused to join either the so-called "congressional" Neolog or the Orthodox faction which had developed in the wake of the unsuccessful Congress of 1868. That Congress aimed at unifying Hungarian Jewry upon the initiative of Baron J. Eötvös, then the Minister of Cults and Public Education.

15. For background information on the issue of Zionism, see R. L. Braham, "Zionism in Hungary," in the *Encyclopedia of Zionism and Israel*, Vol. I, New York, 1971, pp. 523-527.

16. The bickering also continued in the Jewish Council, where the Neolog leaders insisted on strict obedience to the law and the fulfillment of all requirements, while the Orthodox and Zionist leaders occasionally took bolder positions. The dispute between the Neolog and Orthodox leaders was also noted by the Nazis. See: R. L. Braham, *The Destruction of Hungarian Jewry: A Documentary Account*, New York, 1963, Doc. No. 248.

17. For the role of ennobled Jews in Hungary, see O. McCagg, *Jewish Nobles and Geniuses in Modern Hungary*, New York, 1972.

18. Some of the factors underlying the impotence of the traditional Hungarian Jewish leaders during the occupation were also noted by Munkácsi, then Secretary General of the Jewish Community of Pest, and a leading official of the Jewish Council. See his *Hogyan történt*? ("How Did It Happen?"), Budapest, 1947, pp. 10 and 54-55.

19. For details on the Jewish Council in general and its individual members see my: "The Role of the Jewish Council in Hungary: A Tentative Assessment," pp. 69-109.

20. For example, during the middle of June 1944, when the bulk of the provincial Jewish community had already been deported and exterminated, Stern rejected a plan for the clandestine broadcast of "an appeal to the Hungarian Christian society."

21. See his "...'A Race with Time': A Statement," in: *Hungarian-Jewish Studies*, Vol. III, pp. 1-47.

22. *Ibid.*, p. 19.

23. Stern claims that during the deportation of provincial Jewry, Horthy was isolated and still inclined to believe his Minister of the Interior, A. Jaross, who misled him as to the realities of the deportations. *Hungarian Jewish Studies*, Vol. III, p. 17. Also Pető's statement, *ibid.*, p. 55.

24. *Ibid.*, pp. 6-7.

25. *Hungarian Jewish Studies*, Vol. III, pp. 21-22. See also my: "The Role of the Jewish Council in Hungary," pp. 73-74, 102-109.

26. For biographical and other information on Pető and Wilhelm, see *ibid.*, pp. 74-75.

27. The controversial role played by Berend on the Council is beyond the scope of this paper. For further details, see my: "The Role of the Jewish Council in Hungary: A Tentative Assessment." See also Stöckler, "Gettó elött — gettó alatt" ("Before the Ghetto — During the Ghetto"), *Uj Élet*, Budapest, Jan. 22 and 30, Feb. 6, 13, and 20, March 6, and April 17, 1947.

28. The appeals of the Jewish Council were published in the *A Magyar Zsidók Lapja* ("The Bulletin of the Hungarian Jews"), the only paper permitted by the authorities. It was, of course, highly censored, and served primarily as a tool for the manipulation of the Jewish masses.

29. *Ibid.*, April 13, 1944, 1.

30. R. L. Braham, "The Role of the Jewish Council in Hungary," pp. 89, 97-98, and 107.

31. The Rescue Committee of Budapest was established early in 1942, under the auspices of the Rescue Department of the Jewish Agency for Palestine. The Zionist-oriented Budapest Committee, chaired *de facto* by Rezsö Kasztner, was at first primarily concerned with rescuing and assisting the persecuted Jews of Poland and Slovakia. For this purpose, it maintained contact, through couriers, with its counterparts in Bratislava, Geneva, and Istanbul. After the occupation, its leadership, including Joel and Hansi Brand, became preoccupied with the possibility of rescuing Hungarian Jewry by dealing exclusively with the SS. Kasztner's controversial wartime activities became the object of a heated political and legal debate in Israel, where he had settled in 1946. Found guilty by a lower court, he was cleared posthumously—one year after his assassination in Tel Aviv in 1957—by the Israeli Supreme Court. For his own version of his wartime role, see: *Der Bericht des jüdischen Rettungskomitees aus Budapest 1942-1945*, XIII, 1946 (mimeographed). The role played by the unofficial Committee in general, and by its self-appointed volunteer members in particular, is beyond the scope of this paper.

32. For a succinct description of the "Europa-Plan," see my: "The Role of the Jewish Council in Hungary," p. 79.

33. G. Gergely, *Beszámoló a Magyarországi Zsidók Szövetsége Ideiglenes Intéző Bizottsága munkájáról* ("Report on the Work of the Provisional Executive Committee of the Association of the Jews of Hungary"), 1945, p. 5 (manuscript).

34. For examples of favors enjoyed by some of the leaders of Hungarian Jewry, see my: "The Role of the Jewish Council in Hungary," pp. 78-84.

35. In a highly sensational court case involving some leaders of the Judenrat in Będzin, Poland, Chief Justice I. Olshan of the Supreme Court of Israel declared on May 22, 1964, that "no matter how the Judenrat acted, it served the Nazis.... Even those who served the interests of the Jewish communities assisted the Nazis...." *The New York Times*, May 23, 1964. In a document supplementing his testimony in the Eichmann trial, Dán claims that he and Dr. I. Latkoczy were entrusted by the Hungarian Independence Front (*Magyar Függetlenségi Front*) in May 1944 to warn Stern that the Hungarian resistance movement considered the Jewish Council to be a collaborator, and that its members would be considered as war criminals. They allegedly advised Stern that the Council should cease all contacts with the SS Command, and should not issue any more summonses or telegrams requesting Jews to report to work or surrender money, inasmuch as all their efforts were useless, and the trains continued to roll towards Auschwitz. Police of Israel, Bureau 06, Document No. 367.

36. One must note, in this context, that the Hungarian Jews were quite generous to the few thousand Jews who had found refuge in Hungary following their escape from the Third Reich and several Nazi-dominated countries, especially Poland and Slovakia. The Hungarian Jewish agencies primarily concerned with the refugees, as well as with the plight of the poorer stratum of Hungarian Jewry, were the Welfare Bureau of Hungarian Jews (*Magyar Izraeliták Pártfogó Irodája* —MIPI) and its fund-raising arm, the National Hungarian Jewish Assistance Campaign (*Országos Magyar Zsidó Akció* — OMZSA), established in 1938 and 1939 respectively.

6

The Rescue of the Jews of Hungary in Historical Perspective

The destruction of the Jews of Hungary constitutes one of the most perplexing chapters in the history of the Holocaust. Until the German occupation of the country on March 19, 1944, the Jewish community was still relatively intact. While severely restricted in the exercise of their civil and civic rights, the Jews of Hungary lived a comparatively normal life almost oblivious to the destruction that was going on in the neighboring countries. Yet when disaster struck, with the occupation of the country by Germany, this community was subjected—on the very eve of Allied victory—to the most ruthless and concentrated destruction in the Nazis' "Final Solution." Ironically, the destruction of Hungarian Jewry was largely a consequence of the military measures enacted by the Third Reich against a recalcitrant ally that was desperately trying to extricate itself from the Axis alliance.[1]

A number of theological-metaphysical interpreters of the Holocaust have argued that the destruction of Hungarian Jewry ought not to have taken place. By late spring 1944, four and a half years after the beginning of World War II, the leaders of the free world—both Jewish and non-Jewish—were fully familiar with the inner secrets of the "final solution" program. The Allies were advancing triumphantly on all fronts, and the defeat of the Third Reich was only a question of time. Nonetheless, even at this late hour, the destruction process was implemented in Hungary with an efficiency unparalleled in the other parts of German-occupied Europe. Although the Germans came into the country with only contingency plans for a possible "solution" of the Jewish question—they were primarily concerned with assuring

---

Reprinted from *The Historiography of the Holocaust Period*, Yisreal Gutman and Gideon Greif, eds. (Jerusalem: Yad Vashem, 1988) with the permission of the publisher.

Hungary's loyalty and military contribution to the war effort—the SS soon found the climate ideal for the swift and effective implementation of their sinister designs. The number of accomplices they found in Hungary exceeded their wildest expectations, and their early concern about a possible repetition of the Warsaw Uprising was soon assuaged. Despite their awareness of the "final solution," the Hungarian leaders behaved as did their counterparts elsewhere; the Jewish masses, unaware of their fate, were as submissive as the other helpless and defenseless communities caught in the Nazi grip; and the Allied and neutral powers, just as the Vatican and the International Red Cross, continued to manifest their basic indifference toward the Nazis' war against the Jews. A major change in the latter's position came in late June 1944. However, by that time, all of Hungary, with the notable exception of Budapest, was already almost fully *Judenrein.*

The Holocaust in Hungary engendered several controversial questions that agitated and continue to agitate historians and laypersons alike. Why were the SS and their Hungarian accomplices able to carry out their sinister plans? Why weren't the Jewish masses—and the Christian population at large—informed about the realities of Auschwitz? Why did the free world fail to rescue Jews even at that late hour of the war? And why did the Allies refuse to bomb Auschwitz and the rail lines leading to it?

The memoiristic and scholarly and periodical literature dealing with these and other rescue-related questions is one of the richest in the historiography of the Holocaust in Hungary.[2] This historiographical overview, however, will restrict itself to an analytical survey of rescue-related works in general and of those pertaining to the most controversial issues in particular. Among the latter, primary attention will be devoted to writings dealing with "the conspiracy of silence"; the SS-*Vaada* negotiations, including the so-called Europa Plan and the Kasztner-Brand dealings; the so-called Horthy Plan; and the issue of "the bombing of Auschwitz."

Rescue. An Overview of the Literature

During the first few decades of the post-war era, the rescue-related works, like the Holocaust literature in general, were predominantly memoiristic, martyrological, or defensive and apologetic. Many of the authors, both Jewish and non-Jewish, were *dramatis personae* of this tragic era, having played various roles as associates or leaders of official or Underground political, communal or religious organizations. By their very genre, most of these works are subjective, selectively documented, and self-serving. Nevertheless, they contain much valuable information and documentation, which, when used judiciously and in conjunction with other relevant historical sources, constitute an indispensable resource for Holocaust studies. This group of works includes personal narratives by those associated with the central and local Jewish Councils, as well as the accounts by the representatives of the various Christian denominations. Particularly valuable in this category are the memoirs by the former members of the Jewish Council of Budapest.[3]

The accounts by the spokesmen for the Christian churches pertain primarily to the rescue activities undertaken by various orders and convents in Budapest during the Sztójay era in general and the *Nyilas* terror in particular. Many of these exaggerate the rescue achievements of various individuals and institutions. A few are quite critical of the failure of the Christian churches to come to the defense of the Jews both before and after the occupation and for their almost exclusive concern with the welfare of converts.[4] The accounts on the rescue activities of the two Christian institutions established on the initiative and behalf of the converts—the *Szent Kereszt Egylet* (Holy Cross Society) and the *Jó Pásztor Misszió* (Good Shepherd Mission)—are particularly informative, as their authors were themselves mostly converts and naturally more concerned with the plight of the Jews.[5] One can also include in this category the writings pertaining to the rescue activities of the Vatican and of the Budapest Nunciature. While most of these are self-justificatory, a few are openly accusatory.[6] An unexpectedly sympathetic account of the role played by the papacy and its representation in Budapest was provided by Jenö Lévai in 1968.[7]

In recent years a considerable proportion of the periodical literature and monographs dealing with the rescue of Hungarian Jewry has been devoted to the activities of Raoul Wallenberg. The heroic activities of this Swedish diplomat who arrived in Budapest on July 9, 1944, when the Jews of the Hungarian countryside had already been deported, were relatively ignored until the late 1970s. Only one of the limited number of early works on the subject has a solidly scholarly tone.[8] The only other major source that was widely used in Hungarian historiography until recently was Lévai's biographical and somewhat journalistic account.[9] Interest in Wallenberg increased phenomenally since the late 1970s, when Annette and Tom Lantos and other Hungarian-Jewish Americans who had benefited from Wallenberg's rescue activities organized a Concerned Citizens for Wallenberg group. Dedicated to the discovery of Wallenberg's fate in the Soviet Union, where he was taken shortly after his arrest early in 1945, the group acted in concert with many other organizations dedicated to the freeing of Wallenberg. Their collective goal was to focus attention on his rescue activities in Budapest, engendering a veritable avalanche of works of varying quality and usefulness. The claims of many of these authors about Wallenberg's whereabouts and survival in Soviet camps must be accepted with the same skepticism invited by their statistical data relating to the rescued.[10]

For some reason, the rescue activities of Charles Lutz, the late Consul General of the Swiss Legation in Budapest, escaped the attention of journalists and historians. Lutz, who worked closely with the Palestine Office *(Palesztina Hivatal)* and the Chalutz Underground, probably was directly or indirectly responsible for saving as many Jewish lives as Wallenberg.[11] However, a major work doing justice to Lutz has yet to be written.*

Lutz's rescue activities, like those of Wallenberg, were often undertaken in cooperation with the representatives of the International Red Cross in Hungary. This international nongovernmental agency refused, until the summer of 1944, to get directly involved with the rescue of Jews, claiming that it would not be in accordance with the organization's mission as defined by the Geneva Convention of 1929. It reluctantly shifted its stand only after the Swiss press revealed the horrors of the "final solution" in late June 1944—but not before having issued a favorable report on Theresienstadt, the "model concentration camp" visited by its delegation shortly before. The

---

* A German-language work on Lutz appeared in 1986. See Alexander Grossman, *Nur das Gewissen. Carl Lutz und seine Budapester Aktion. Geschichte und Porträt* (Wald: Im Waldgut, 1986), 284 p.

performance of the International Red Cross in Hungary has not yet been adequately explored.* The relatively few published journalistic accounts are generally superficial and constitute only a modest foundation for a historian interested in the subject matter.[12] Most of the comprehensive works on the Holocaust, especially those dealing with the destruction of Hungarian Jewry, contain succinct though generally more fully documented accounts.[13] Both of these source groups are critical of the war-time performance of the International Red Cross pertaining to the Jews.

One of the major havens of rescue, especially for the Jews of Northern Transylvania, was Romania. Only a limited number of Jews took advantage of this opportunity, primarily because they were unaware of the ultimate fate awaiting them. The stories of those who were rescued, the diplomatic and political activities connected with the Romanian authorities, and the Underground activities of Jewish rescuers on both sides of the border are detailed in a limited number of works. Almost all of them are quite sympathetic about Romania's posture toward the plight of the Jews of Hungary in 1944.[14]

Not many of the comprehensive works and documentary collections treat the rescue of Hungarian Jewry in any detail. By far the most useful ones that appeared shortly after the war are the two volumes by Lévai. Dealing with domestic and foreign rescue efforts, respectively, these books, though largely journalistic and non-analytical, contain a considerable number of historically valuable documents that for a long time were not otherwise available to researchers interested in the Holocaust in Hungary.[15] Analytical-scholarly collections of documents containing several chapters dealing with various domestic and foreign involvements in rescue were published in the 1960s.[16] The first comprehensive scholarly historical account on the Holocaust in Hungary, which devotes separate sections to all aspects of domestic and international, Jewish and non-Jewish, governmental and nongovernmental, rescue efforts, appeared in the early 1980s.[17] The bulk of the rescue-related literature, both scholarly

* A solid study on the subject matter was published in 1988. See Arieh Ben-Tov, *Facing the Holocaust in Budapest: The International Committee of the Red Cross and the Jews of Hungary, 1943-1945* (Boston: M. Nijhoff, 1988), 492 p.

and polemical, emphasizes the major controversies that arose in connection with the Holocaust in Hungary.

The Conspiracy of Silence

Perhaps the most explosive issue for historians in recent years has revolved around the question: "Who knew what, and what did those who knew and were able to act do?" With respect to Hungary, the first dispassionate and fully documented overview, carefully differentiating between facts, claims, and assumptions, was presented by this author in a lengthy paper for an international conference on *The Holocaust—A Generation After* in New York (1975). The paper aimed to demonstrate, among other things, that the leaders of Hungary were acquainted with the details of the massacres perpetrated by the Einsatzgruppen in the Axis-occupied parts of the Soviet Union—including the murder of close to 20,000 "alien" Jews from Hungary near Kamenets Podolski in 1941—and that of the Jewish leaders in particular were kept abreast of the anti-Jewish campaign in Nazi-dominated Europe via a variety of Jewish and non-Jewish intelligence sources. The author further demonstrates that by early spring 1944, weeks before the beginning of the mass deportations in Hungary, the leaders of Hungary, like those of the free world, had absolute proof about the realities of Auschwitz. Yet they failed either to inform the Jewish masses or to enlighten the Christian population about the impending fate of the deportees.[18] Similar conclusions, beyond the scope of Hungary alone, were also reached by Hannah Arendt,[19] Walter Laqueur,[20] and Martin Gilbert.[21] The latter two, both widely recognized authorities, devote special attention to the basic indifference of the Allies during the war, providing a variety of well-reasoned assumptions and explanations.

The conspiracy of silence in the destruction of Hungarian Jewry has acquired a special importance in the recent writings of John S. Conway.[22] Conway argues persuasively that the Hungarian deportees, like the Jews elsewhere in Nazi-dominated Europe, had no inkling about the terrible end that awaited them. However, he aims to demonstrate that one—if not the basic—reason for this tragedy was the unenviable position adopted by the Slovak Jewish leaders in the course of their negotiations with the SS in 1942-1943, a position with which the Hungarian Jewish leaders, especially the Zionist ones, were not only acquainted but also adopted subsequent to the German occupation. Relying to a large extent on the views and evidence presented by Rudolf Vrba (Walter Rosenberg),[23] one of the escapees from Auschwitz, who emerged as a leading critic of the Jewish leaders' complacency during the war, and Ladislav Lipscher, the author of a well-documented account of the destruction of Slovakia's Jewry,[24] Conway argues that the Slovak Jewish leaders constituting the so-called Working Group in the central Jewish Council found themselves in a highly compromised position soon after the first deportations left Slovakia.[25] Having—albeit against their will—cooperated with the Germans and their Slovak accomplices in the expropriation and deportation of a large number of Slovak Jews soon after the death camps were made operative early in 1942, they learned almost immediately about the realities of the "resettlement" program. One of the deportees, Dionys Lenard, managed to return to Slovakia within a month and allegedly informed the Jewish leaders about what was going on in Majdanek.

The Jewish leaders, Conway continues, already had considerable experience in freeing individual Jews, mostly well-to-do or prominent persons, from the harsh work camps in Slovakia by bribing the appropriate German and Slovak officials. After Lenard's report, they decided to approach Dieter Wisliceny, the head of the Sonderkommando in charge of the deportations from Slovakia, with a bribe offer. The basic reason for the contact, Conway concludes, was the same in Hungary as in Slovakia. He notes that the patterns followed on the Nazi as well as the Jewish side were

> too similar to be merely accidental. Indeed the parallels are striking in the readiness of certain members of the Jewish Councils of both countries to enter into secret negotiations with the Germans, in their belief in the possibility of rescuing themselves and a few select members of the Jewish community, or at least of obtaining a delay in their own favor from the Nazis or the local authorities, in their willingness to suppress their knowledge of the mass murders, and in their deliberate failure to inform the victims of their probable fate.

While this linkage theory is dramatic and has considerable merit, it is, in the view of this author at least, based largely on conjecture.

Lenard's revelations notwithstanding, the "proof" of the "final solution" was not as substantiated in 1942 or 1943 as it was in 1944—at least for the Jewish leaders in Nazi-dominated Europe. The illusion that the remnant of Slovakian Jewry would be saved, even after 52,000, or two-thirds of the community, had been deported by June 1942, was not totally unfounded. The deportations were indeed halted shortly after Wisliceny was given $20,000, but the Slovak Jewish leaders had no way of knowing the truth behind that decision. As this author demonstrated in another context, this decision by the Nazis was based on tactical considerations.

Wisliceny and his colleagues had been confronted with a dilemma. The national leaders of Slovakia, like many others, including the Papal Nuncio, when informed about the true purpose of the deportations, had asked the Germans for an opportunity to visit the new Jewish "settlements" in Poland. Granting the request would have jeopardized the "final solution" program that was then being implemented in many other parts of Nazi-dominated Europe. Berlin was therefore advised to suspend, at least temporarily, the deportations from Slovakia.[26]

In contrast to the decisive importance attached by Conway and many other historians to the "conspiracy of silence" in the destruction of Hungarian Jewry, Yehuda Bauer tends to minimize this factor, arguing that the secret was not a monopoly of the leaders. Using a sophisticated semantic-epistemological argument, differentiating between "information" and "knowledge," Bauer insists that the proponents of the conspiracy theory "misread the whole historical situation." The Hungarian Jews, he argues, did not have to rely on their leaders for information on the "final solution," for

> that information was there all the time, including the information regarding the ways in which the Nazis were misleading and fooling their victims. The point is that this information was rejected, people did not *want* to know, because knowledge would have caused pain and suffering, and there was seemingly no way out.[27]

While this position is obviously based on the accounts of Chalutz Underground figures who visited some of the provincial ghettos, it goes counter to the personal narratives, both written and taped, of almost all the survivors of the Holocaust in Hungary. There is no doubt that some Chalutz couriers did indeed inform the leaders of the Jewish communities that they visited, and perhaps even some groups of Jews, about the fate which awaited them, but communications by totally unknown zealous youngsters simply would not have been accepted as reliable information, let alone absorbed as knowledge, when they conflicted with the official communications transmitted by the trusted traditional Jewish leadership in Budapest.

The controversy over the failure to rescue Hungarian Jewry on the eve of the Allied victory acquires a special dimension in connection with the negotiations with the SS, which were initiated by the Bratislava Working Group and continued by its Budapest counterpart.

The SS – Working Group Negotiations

The reasons for the involvement of the SS in negotiations with the Working Group leaders are now well documented. As the fortunes of the war changed, late in 1942, following the staggering losses suffered by the Axis forces, the Nazis became eager to expand the Waffen-SS. Toward this end they expressed a readiness to free *individual Jews* in return for substantial sums of hard currency—an objective for which Himmler allegedly also received Hitler's blessing.[28] But the Working Group of Bratislava was convinced that the deportations from Slovakia had been halted because of their bribing of Wisliceny; therefore they extended the frame of their negotiations in October 1942 to include the other persecuted Jewish communities of Europe. The Europa Plan, as this scheme came to be known, called for the suspension of the deportations of Jews to Poland in exchange for the payment of $2 million. These negotiations continued into 1943, when, following the defeat at Stalingrad, the military outlook of the Third Reich became quite bleak. The framework of this grandiose rescue plan was extended to Hungary almost immediately after the occupation. Wisliceny, equipped with a persuasive "letter of recommendation" from Rabbi Michael Dov Weissmandel, a leading member of the Working Group, first got in touch with Fülöp Freudiger, the representative of the Orthodox community in the Jewish Council of Budapest, and then with the leaders of the Zionist-dominated Budapest Vaada, including Rudolf (Rezsö) Kasztner.

The SS-Jewish negotiations and deals for the possible rescue of the Jews of Hungary have given rise to heated arguments among historians as well as laypersons, especially survivors.

Strong partisans may be found on both sides of the barricades. On one side are the memoirs and reports of the Jewish *dramatis personae,* including Andreas Biss, Joel Brand, and Kasztner which—like those written by their Slovak counterparts—are very tendentious and apologetic. They uniformly attempt to justify their own positions, emphasize their successes, and place the blame for failure primarily on the Western Allies and the Jewish leaders of the free world, especially Saly Mayer, the AJDC representative in Switzerland.[29] A similar viewpoint is expressed by a few "outside" supporters, some of whom were beneficiaries of the rescue activities.

Many authors, on the other hand, are critical, even to the point of being caustic. The case against the Budapest Vaada leaders, and indirectly against some of their closest associates in the provinces and in Budapest, was presented by Jews and non-Jews, private individuals and government officials, professionals and laymen using a variety of political-ideological, historical-moral, and judicial arguments. Many of them base their conclusions on the memoirs of Adolf Eichmann (who claimed, among other things, that he had had a "gentleman's agreement," under which Kasztner allegedly offered to remain silent in return for the opportunity to rescue a few "biologically valuable" Jews),[30] Judge Benjamin Halevi's now-famous contention that Kasztner had "sold his soul to the devil," and Vrba's harsh indictment of the Zionist leaders of Slovakia and Hungary. Perhaps one of the best illustrations of this genre of literature is *Perfidy* by Ben Hecht (who had, of course, his own Revisionist axe to grind).[31]

The anti-Zionist critics of the Budapest Vaada's rescue activities include two strange bedfellows: some elements of the Neturei Karta, the ultra-Orthodox Jewish group, and the Communists. Among the former, by far the most scathing attack on the Zionists is included in Reb Moshe Schoenfeld's *The Holocaust Victims Accuse*.[32] The Vaada leaders are accused not only of having tried to rescue only themselves and their political allies, but also of having been more concerned with laying the foundations of the future Jewish state than with the immediate problems of rescue. In this respect, their views parallel those of the Irgun, which directed its ire against the Jewish establishment in the free world.

Soviet authors and their counterparts in some of the Soviet bloc nations have published vicious and obscene accusations. As part of their vitriolic campaign against Israel, these authors, clearly supported by their parties and governments, not only denigrate the Holocaust, but also fan the flames of anti-Semitism through their thinly disguised attacks on Zionism and cosmopolitanism. They portray the activities of the Budapest Vaada as closely synchronized with those of the Nazis and directed against the interests of the Jewish masses. An example of this genre of Communist literature is Yuri Ivanov's *Caution: Zionism!*[33] Another basic characteristic of this literature, especially that dealing with rescue and resistance in Hungary, is an almost complete silence about the involvement of the Chalutz youth in rescue and anti-Nazi Underground activities and the elevation to the level of legend of the few sporadic operations initiated and carried out under the leadership of the illegal Communist Party.[34]

An interesting though not totally convincing thesis about the Working Group's Europa Plan and the subsequent "blood for trucks" mission of Joel Brand is offered by Yehuda Bauer. Relying to a large extent on Weissmandel's account, Bauer concludes that the Germans took the Europa Plan seriously, for, as the Working Group leaders reportedly argued, "the bait was obviously not the paltry sum of money but the prospect of contacts with Weissmandel's 'world of rabbis'." The Nazis, says Bauer, citing Weissmandel in substantiation of his position, were not only interested in money: "They wanted in this way to get in touch with Jews in the U.S. for some political reason that was more important to them than the extermination of the Jews."[35]

The political reason, which was soon discovered to have also been military in nature, was first revealed by Bela Vago in his perceptive piece on "The Intelligence Aspects of the Brand Mission."[36] Based on the minutes of the British interrogation of Brand and Andor ("Bandi") Grosz—the shady character and multiple spy the Nazis selected to accompany Brand—Vago carefully speculates on the possible ulterior motives of the Germans; although he is mindful of the fact that Grosz's testimony has to be taken with a grain of salt in view of his well-founded personal reasons for shading the truth.

Bauer's apparent linkage of Weissmandel's account with Grosz's testimony lent itself to the conclusion that the *real* mission was assigned by the Nazis to Grosz and that Brand was only sent along to provide a convenient cover. Grosz's alleged mission was part of a greater plan reflecting the desire of the top leadership of the Reich Security Main Office, including Heinrich Himmler and Walter Schellenberg, to establish contact with the Western Allies. By that time, according to this reasoning, these top Nazis were already convinced that the war was lost and were ready, even against the will of Hitler, to sign a separate peace treaty. This objective, according to Bauer, was reinforced by the awareness of the *Reichsführer-SS* "that a strong, conservative opposition was bent on trying to eliminate Hitler."[37]

Bauer fails to identify, let alone resolve, the obvious dilemma: if Himmler and his cohorts aimed, behind Hitler's back, to establish a separate peace with the Western Allies through Jewish contacts—a goal that was purportedly "more important for them than the extermination of Jews"—why was Hungarian Jewry, two days *before* the departure of the Brand-Grosz mission on May 17, 1944, subjected to the most ruthless and concentrated destruction process of the war? If Himmler was so serious in the pursuit of his grandiose covert plans, why was he so relentless in the pursuit of the "final solution" in Hungary—a country whose Jews allegedly represented such an important bargaining chip—to the point that he even sacrificed the interests of the Wehrmacht by transferring the freight-cars so desperately needed by the war effort for use in the deportation of those very Jews?

The answer, according to this author at least, lies elsewhere. The Nazis were never serious about allowing any major groups of Jews to escape their clutches. They single-mindedly pursued their racially and ideologically defined objectives: the total liquidation of European Jewry during the war. The negotiations with the Jewish leaders served multiple purposes: (a) to raise false hopes in the Budapest Vaada and among other Jewish leaders, who were basically powerless though desperate to save as many Jewish lives as possible by freeing individuals or smaller groups of Jews;[38] (b) to induce these leaders to lull the Jewish masses into submission; (c) to acquire Jewish wealth, including hard currency and industrial establishments;[39] (d) to drive a wedge in the Grand Alliance by provocatively courting the Western Allies; and (e) to provide alibis for the post-war era.[40]

Yehuda Bauer's position with regard to the Europa Plan has been countered by Livia Rothkirchen, an authority on the Holocaust in Slovakia, in a perceptive piece reassessing her own previously held views on the plan.[41] While Himmler may have had some ideas about the possible extrication of the Third Reich when the *Götterdämmerung* loomed on the horizon, he never lost his zeal for the successful completion of the "final solution."

The fact that the various rescue plans, negotiations, and missions were never seriously considered by the Nazis is clearly demonstrated by the views and instructions Himmler communicated to his subordinates in 1944. According to Kurt Becher, one of the chief negotiators with the Budapest Vaada leaders, Himmler had urged him to "get from the Jews whatever is possible. Squeeze, promise them what they ask for. What shall be kept of this promise, we shall see."[42] On July 31, 1944, when only the Jews of Budapest were still left in the country, Himmler was eager to impress *Gauleiter* Martin Mutschmann with his resolve to use the "requisite toughness" to complete the "final solution" in Hungary. It was in the same vein that he communicated with Rudolf Höss in the fall of 1944, emphasizing that the extermination program "will continue to be carried out and will be intensified month by month...."[43]

The Bombing of Auschwitz and the Horthy Offer

The writers who are convinced that the various SS negotiations might have been successful have found ample, and perhaps more justifiable, reasons also to blame the Western Allies for the failure of the other two schemes designed to save Hungarian Jewry. In this they were joined by many other reputable authors. The indifference of the United States and Great Britain to the plight of the Jews in Nazi-dominated Europe has been well documented by Henry Feingold, Martin Gilbert, Walter Laqueur, Arthur Morse, Bernard Wasserstein, and David Wyman.[44] Some of these authors were quite objective about the motivations of the Allied leaders and appreciate their efforts toward indirectly helping the Jews by their military drive against the Third Reich; others emphasize the negative aspects of the Allied position. Adopting a moralistic-utopian approach in their analysis of international affairs, most of these authors ignore or denigrate the basic motivation in the behavior of nations, especially in the nation-state system of the world: the pursuit of national interests, which is usually defined in terms of power.

The bombing of Auschwitz and of the rail lines leading to it became an issue in the wake of the request forwarded by Jewish sources to the Western Allies in early June 1944. It is not absolutely clear whether the idea originated with Rabbi Weissmandel or the two Slovak Jews who had escaped from Auschwitz. The first documented account of why the Allies rejected the suggestion was offered by Wyman.[45] A more fully elaborated and well-reasoned description and analysis of the Western Allies' position were later provided by Gilbert.[46]

While virtually all the authors[47] condemn the Western Allies and provide basically the same explanation for the failure to bomb Auschwitz despite the proven ability to do so, none of them extends his critical inquiry to the Soviet Union, which at the time—when the Red Army had already crossed the Dniester—was strategically in a much better position to bomb not only Auschwitz but all the death camps. Equally neglected is the record of the resistance forces and of the Jewish Underground including the Chalutz youth. There is no evidence that these anti-Nazi elements sabotaged any of the rail lines used for the deportation of the Hungarian Jews! Questions are not raised about the failure of the Jewish leaders to advance such requests *before* June 1944, by which time not only many European Jewish communities but also most of the provincial Jews of Hungary had already been liquidated.

Conway takes issue also with the critics of the Allies. He argues that the bombing of the death camps or of the rail lines would not have prevented the Germans from completing their "final solution," as they had ample slave labor to quickly repair the lines and, if the gas chambers and crematoria had been destroyed, they could have used other—though less efficient—means to liquidate the Jews. His inescapable conclusion is that "the idea of bombing Auschwitz in order to prevent the murder of any further Hungarian or other victims, was the product of wishful thinking."[48]

The indifference of the Western Allies is demonstrated by most of these authors in connection with the so-called Horthy offer. This offer to allow the emigration of a number of Hungarian Jews was based on a rescue scheme initiated by the Budapest Palestine Office headed by Miklós Krausz, in conjunction with Charles Lutz. It was made shortly after the suspension of deportations on July 7, 1944, when the countryside was already *Judenrein,* and involved 7,800 Jews. Three to four hundred were sponsored by the Swedes, and around 7,000, holders of Palestine immigration certificates or British offers of admission, were sponsored by the Swiss. Many writers mistakenly state that approximately 40,000 Jews were officially involved in the offer—a figure they apparently cite from each other. They are evidently unaware that this figure was occasionally used by Krausz in his tactics to save as many Jews as possible. Krausz unilaterally decided that the 7,800 Swedish and Swiss, i.e., British, permits were for heads of families and, as such, covered around 40,000 Jews. This, however, was accepted neither by the Hungarians nor the others involved in the negotiations.

Horthy's offer was approved by Hitler under certain conditions. On July 10, 1944, heeding the advice of Joachim von Ribbentrop and Edmund Veesenmayer, his plenipotentiary in Hungary, Hitler consented to the emigration of these Jews, *"provided the Hungarians allowed the speedy resumption of the deportation of the remaining [i.e., Budapest] Jews"* (italics added).[49] The Germans never intended, of course, to permit the emigration of even the limited number of Jews. Acting in collusion with Himmler, Eichmann was resolved—once the Hungarians accepted Hitler's conditions—"to carry out the expected expulsion of the Jews from Budapest once it is proceeded with, with the utmost suddenness and with such speed that they will be driven out before anyone has had a chance to obtain a travel document or visa to a foreign country."[50] That the Germans were not really serious in allowing larger groups of Jews to escape their clutches is also revealed by the documents in the archives of Charles Lutz at Yad Vashem.[51]

The evidence is not clear whether the Americans and the British were aware of this German position. In any case, although the British were concerned with their position in Palestine and sensitive to the aspirations of the Arabs in the Middle East, they finally yielded to the recommendations of the Americans, who were then in the midst of a presidential campaign.[52] On August 17, 1944, they issued a joint declaration that was communicated to the Hungarians via the International Red Cross. The Western Allies expressed their readiness to accept Horthy's offer, emphasizing, however, that their generosity should not be construed as condoning "the action of the Hungarian Government in forcing the emigration of Jews as an alternative to persecution and death." They placed the burden of arranging for the actual emigration on Hungary and Germany, but declared themselves ready to take care of all those who reached neutral or United Nations territory.

Although the collective passports were duly processed by the Swiss and the exit visas were granted by the Hungarian officials, nothing came of the emigration scheme. The Germans, acting in collusion with their radical Hungarian Right accomplices, refused to grant free passage unless the Hungarians first fulfilled Hitler's precondition.

The indictment of the Western Allies for this "missed opportunity of rescue" is somewhat gratuitous. There is no doubt that the members of the Grand Alliance, not to speak of the neutral world, could have done much more to alleviate the plight of the Jews—in Hungary and elsewhere in Europe. However, the Horthy offer, like the rescue schemes pursued by the Budapest Vaada, came to naught not because the West had failed—as Bauer concluded in connection with the Brand mission—but because a racially and ideologically obsessed great military power was bent on achieving at least one of its major objectives of the war: the final solution of the Jewish question in Europe.

NOTES

1. For details on the background of the occupation, see Randolph L. Braham, *The Politics of Genocide. The Holocaust in Hungary* (hereafter, RLB), New York, 1981, pp. 362-377.

2. Randolph L. Braham, *The Hungarian Jewish Catastrophe. A Selected and Annotated Bibliography*, 2d. rev. and enl. ed. (hereafter, *Bibliography)*, New York, 1984, refs. no. 1396-1632.

3. See the accounts by Fülöp Freudiger, Ottó Komoly, Ernö Petö, and Samu Stern in *Hungarian-Jewish Studies*, vol. 3, Randolph L. Braham, ed., New York, 1973. For

references to other pertinent accounts and commentaries about the rescue activities of the Council, see *Bibliography*, refs. no. 535-571.

4. Particularly valuable are the following works: Albert Bereczky, *Hungarian Protestantism and the Persecution of the Jews*, Budapest, 1946; *A magyar katolikus egyház és az emberi jogok védelme* (The Hungarian Roman Catholic Church and the Protection of Human Rights), Antal Meszlényi, ed., Budapest, 1947; László T. László, *Az egyházak szerepe a zsidómentésben Magyarországon* (The Churches' Role in the Saving of Jews in Hungary), *Katolikus Szemle* (Catholic Review), Rome, vol. 31, no. 2, 1979, pp. 139-163 and no. 3, 1979, pp. 217-235. For other relevant sources see *Bibliography*, refs. no. 1551-1623.

5. *Ibid.*, refs. no. 1581-1582, 1621-1623.

6. *Ibid.*, refs. no. 1624-1632.

7. Jenö Lévai, *Hungarian Jewry and the Papacy*, London, 1968.

8. G.B. Freed [George Barany], "Humanitarianism vs. Totalitarianism: The Strange Case of Raoul Wallenberg," *Papers of the Michigan Academy of Science, Arts, and Letters*, vol. 46, 1961, pp. 503-528.

9. *Raoul Wallenberg regényes élete hösi küzdelmei, rejtélyes eltünésének titka* (Raoul Wallenberg's Adventurous Life, Heroic Struggles and the Secret of His Mysterious Disappearance), Budapest, 1948.

10. *See Bibliography*, refs. no. 1471-1501. Perhaps the best account in this category is Elenore Lester, *Wallenberg. The Man in the Iron Web*, Englewood Cliffs, N.J., 1982.

11. See *Bibliography*, refs. no. 1505-1506. For a valuable reference work giving an indication of Lutz's involvement in the rescue of Hungarian Jewry, see Bronia Klibanski, "Archives of the Swiss Consul General Charles Lutz," *Yad Vashem Studies*, Vol. XV, Jerusalem, 1983, pp. 357-366. For a succinct overview of Lutz's activities in Hungary, see *RLB*, pp. 1077-1083.

12. *Bibliography*, refs. no. 1460-1462; see also RLB, pp. 905-913.

13. *Ibid.*, refs. no. 437-452; see especially RLB, pp. 1057-1063.

14. *Bibliography*, refs no. 1460-1462; see also RLB, pp. 905-913.

15. See his *Szürke könyv magyar zsidók megmentéséröl* (Grey Book on the Rescuing of Hungarian Jews), Budapest, 1946; and *Fehér könyv. Külföldi akciók zsidók megmentésére* (White Book. Foreign Actions for the Rescuing of Jews), Budapest, 1946.

16. See, for example, Randolph L. Braham, *The Destruction of Hungarian Jewry. A Documentary Account*, New York, 1963; see especially Docs. 324-437.

17. See RLB, *op. cit.*

18. The paper by Randolph L. Braham was reproduced in an abbreviated form in *The Holocaust as Historical Experience*, Yehuda Bauer and Nathan Rottenstreich, eds., New York, 1980, pp. 109-131. An expanded version appeared in RLB, pp. 691-731.

19. *Eichmann in Jerusalem. A Report on the Banality of Evil*, New York, 1963.

20. *The Terrible Secret. Suppression of the Truth About Hitler's "Final Solution,"* Boston, 1980.

21. *Auschwitz and the Allies*, New York, 1982.

22. "Frühe Augenzeugenberichte aus Auschwitz. Glaubwürdigkeit und Wirkungsgeschichte," *Vierteljahrshefte für Zeitgeschichte*, Munich, vol. 27, no. 2, April 1979, pp. 260-284.

23. See his and Alan Bestic's *I Cannot Forgive*, New York, 1964.

24. *Die Juden im Slovakischen Staat, 1939-1945*, Munich-Vienna, 1980.

25. Conway's views were documented in a manuscript, "The Holocaust in Hungary. Recent Controversies and Reconsiderations," scheduled for publication in *Vierteljahrshefte für Zeitgeschichte.*

26. RLB, pp. 937-938.

27. See Bauer, *The Holocaust in Historical Perspective*, Seattle, 1978, p. 106. Bauer's major source for his position is Josef Shefer, "The Leadership of the Halutz Underground in Hungary," see *Bibliography*, ref. no. 1365.

28. Livia Rothkirchen, "The ' Europa Plan': A Reassessment" in *American Jewry and the Holocaust* by Seymour M. Finger, New York, May 1984, Appendix 4-7, offset.

29. *Bibliography*, refs. no. 1406, 1407, 1412, 1414, 1423, and 1428.

30. "Eichmann Tells His Own Damning Story." *Life*, vol. 49, no. 23, December 5, 1960, p. 146.

31. *See Bibliography*, ref. no. 1918.

32. *Ibid.*, ref. no. 1924.

33. *Ibid.*, ref. no. 1919.

34. *Ibid.*, refs. no. 1313-1341.

35. See Bauer, *A History of the Holocaust*, New York, 1982, p. 311.

36. *Bibliography*, ref. no. 1427.

37. See *A History of the Holocaust, op. cit.*, pp. 942-943. This theme is further elaborated in *The Holocaust in Historical Perspective, op. cit.*, pp. 94-171.

38. It is in this category that one can include the so-called Kasztner transports, which also included the approximately eighty provincial Jewish leaders freed through Freudiger's negotiations with Wisliceny, the escape of Freudiger and his family, and the placement of some 21,000 Jews "on ice" in Strasshof. For details on these rescue successes, see RLB, pp. 426-427, 649-653, 791-792, 952-968.

39. The acquisition of the Weiss-Manfréd Works, Hungary's largest industrial complex, by freeing about forty members of the owners' families falls into this category. For details see RLB, pp. 514-524; see also *Bibliography*, refs. no. 600-606.

40. RLB, pp. 930-986.

41. See footnote 28.

42. Testimony of Kurt Andreas Becher, Bremen, June 20, 1961, Eichmann Trial, Document T., p. 12, as quoted by Livia Rothkirchen in "The 'Europa Plan': A Reassessment," *op. cit.*, p. 16.

43. *Ibid.*

44. *Bibliography*, refs. no. 561, 1437, 1456, 1510, and 1513.

45. "Why Auschwitz Was Never Bombed," *Commentary*, New York, May 1978, pp. 37-46. An updated version is included in David S. Wyman, *The Abandonment of the Jews. America and the Holocaust, 1941-1945*, New York, 1984.

46. *Auschwitz and the Allies*, New York, 1982.

47. See also *Bibliography*, refs. no. 1436-1445.

48. See *The Holocaust in Hungary: Recent Controversies and Reconsiderations, op. cit.*

49. See RLB, pp. 1077-1083.

50. *Ibid.*

51. See footnote 11.

52. For some details on the Horthy Offer and the attitudes of the Western Allies, see *Bibliography*, refs. no. 1439, 2455, and 1456.

7

The National Trials Relating to the Holocaust in Hungary: An Overview

Background

It is generally recognized that the Holocaust in Hungary, the last major chapter in the Nazis' war against the Jews, was unique—a chapter replete with paradoxes and controversies. While the Jewish communities throughout the rest of German-dominated Europe were being systematically destroyed, the Jews of Hungary—although subjected to severe discriminatory measures and occasional physical abuse—continued to enjoy the protection of the conservative-aristocratic government until the German occupation on March 19, 1944. After the occupation, however, it was this highly assimilated patriotic Jewish community that was subjected to the most ruthless destruction program of the war. The occupation enabled the German and Hungarian Nazis, each previously eager but unable to act alone, to unite their forces in carrying out the Final Solution at lightning speed. What took years to implement in other parts of Europe, took only a few months in Hungary! By July 9, all of Hungary, with the notable exception of Budapest, had become *Judenrein*.[1] The destruction of the Hungarian Jews took place on the eve of Allied victory, when the secrets of Auschwitz were already widely known.[2] Except for a few diehard Nazis who continued to believe Hitler's promises about new wonder weapons, even the perpetrators realized the defeat of the Axis was inevitable. The imminent military defeat notwithstanding—or precisely because of it—the perpetrators became even more committed to winning at least the genocidal war against the Jews. They won

---

Scheduled for publication in *Law, Religion and the Evolution of Holocaust Scholarship*, Marshall M. Lee and Larry Thompson, eds. (Evanston, IL: Northwestern University Press, 2000). Printed with the permission of the editors.

this phase of the war in Hungary because the Quisling government of Döme Sztójay, installed with the blessing of Regent Miklós Horthy a few days after the German occupation, placed the instruments of state power—the police, the gendarmerie, and the civil service—at their disposal. While not always enthusiastic, the policemen, gendarmes, and civil servants operating at the various levels of government carried out the Final Solution—the isolation, expropriation, ghettoization, concentration, and deportation of the Jews—with a routine and an efficiency that impressed even the Eichmann-*Sonderkommando*. The latter, numbering less than 200 SS-men, clearly could not have carried out the program without the wholehearted cooperation of the Hungarians.[3]

As the Soviet forces advanced westward toward Hungary, many thousands of the perpetrators fled in the same direction, together with countless other fascists. Many among them managed to escape altogether; others were captured by the British or the Americans in occupied Austria and Germany. Quite a few of the latter managed to hide their criminal background and ended up in various parts of the free world, especially Argentina, Australia, Britain, Canada, and the United States, where they lived out their lives—or continue to live—undetected, having capitalized on their credentials as reliable anti-communists during the Cold War.[4] The major Hungarian war criminals who had played a leadership role in the various pro-Nazi governments and political parties and had been actively involved in the planning and implementation of the anti-Jewish measures could not hide their background. Once they became the target of special investigative efforts, those among the Hungarian governmental and political figures in Allied hands were easily unmasked. The same happened to a number of top German officials with whom they had collaborated during the occupation.

The postwar Hungarian government requested that the Western Allies arrest and extradite 483 Hungarians and 38 Germans suspected as war criminals. The Hungarian demands for the extradition of these criminals, especially those of German nationality, caused considerable friction between the Hungarian and American authorities.[5] The tensions were eased when 390 of the Hungarian suspects were returned and the Americans consented to the extradition of three top SS officials who had been active during the occupation to serve as witnesses in the major Hungarian war crimes trials. These were *SS-Brigadeführer* Edmund Veesenmayer, Hitler's Plenipotentiary; *SS-Obergruppenführer* Otto Winkelmann, the Higher SS and Police Leader; and *SS-Standartenführer* Kurt Becher, Heinrich Himmler's "economic" representative.[6]

The major Hungarian war criminals were rounded up and first interrogated by a team headed by Martin Himmler, a Hungarian-American who headed the Hungarian Section of the Office of Strategic Services in Salzburg, Austria. Most of these were returned to Hungary in October 1945, escorted by Lieutenant George Granville, an American Air Force officer of Hungarian background. Among these were practically all the leading figures of the Sztójay and Szálasi governments. Upon their return to Budapest, they were handed over to Major-General Gábor Péter, the head of the Political Police (*Politikai Rendészeti Osztály*).[7]

Of the three Germans extradited by the Western Allies to serve as prosecution witnesses only Veesenmayer was eventually tried (see below). Many other German and Austrian nationals who had been involved in the Hungarian chapter of the Nazis' Final Solution, however, were tried elsewhere. Among the most important of these trials were those held in Germany, Austria, Czechoslovakia, and Israel. A number of Hungarian nationals, in turn, were tried outside of Hungary, including Romania, Yugoslavia, the United States, and Canada. Some, like those who were tried in Yugoslavia, were extradited by the Hungarian government; others, many of whom had originally been tried *in absentia* in Hungary, were placed on trial abroad after being unmasked.

Hungary

By far the most important trials relating to the destruction of Hungarian Jewry were those held in Hungary. Many of the accused, especially people suspected of having been active in the roundup, ghettoization, and deportation of the Jews, were tried in the appropriate county's People's Tribunal. The major war criminals, i.e., those who had served in top government positions and collaborated with the SS and other German agencies in the planning and implementation of the Final Solution, were tried in Budapest.

The courts involved in the trials operated in accordance with the provisions of Article 14 of the Armistice Agreement of January 20, 1945, under which Hungary undertook to cooperate in the apprehension and trial of persons accused of war crimes and crimes against humanity. In compliance with these provisions, the Provisional National Government adopted Decree No. 81/1945.M.E. (January 25, 1945), establishing a system of "people's courts." These were envisioned to function until a duly elected legislature could set up a permanent court system.[8] Under the Decree, two types of courts were established: (1) People's Tribunals (*népbíróságok*), lower trial courts that functioned in most county seats, with each court presided over by a professional judge acting in conjunction with five lay judges or "people's assessors."[9] (2) The National Council of People's Tribunals (*A Népbíróságok Országos Tanácsa*—NOT) which heard appeals from the People's Tribunals. NOT was headed by a professional judge appointed by the Minister of Justice and operated through several appellate councils, each consisting of five professional judges working in conjunction with lay deputies representing the coalition parties.[10]

The trials of the major war criminals began shortly after their extradition by the Western Allies. Even before their return to Budapest, however, so-called "revolutionary courts" tried and convicted a number of Hungarian officers and guards who had committed horrendous crimes against labor servicemen (*munkaszolgálatosok*), especially in the Ukraine and Serbia.[11]

The series of trials involving the major war criminals began in Budapest on October 29, 1945. The first to be tried was former Prime Minister László Bárdossy. During his 11-month tenure as Premier (April 1941-March 1942), Hungary participated in the invasion of Yugoslavia, declared war on the Soviet Union and the USA, and became firmly committed to the Third Reich. It was also during his premiership that Hungary adopted the third major anti-Jewish law (clearly based on the Nazis' Nuremberg Law of 1935), exacerbated the Jewish labor service system, rounded up and deported close to 18,000 "alien" Jews (most of whom were slaughtered near Kamenets-Podolsk in late August 1941), and witnessed the massacre of close to a thousand Jews (along with 3,000 Serbs) by Hungarian army and gendarmerie units in the Bácska area in January-February 1942.[12] Convicted on November 3, Bárdossy was executed by a firing squad on January 10, 1946, following his unsuccessful appeal to NOT.[13]

Bárdossy's trial was followed by that of former Prime Minister Béla Imrédy. He was accused of crimes associated with his involvement in pro-Reich and anti-Jewish activities during his brief tenure as premier (May 1938-February 1939) and especially in connection with his services in the Quisling government of Döme Sztójay. Originally an Anglophile, Imrédy was indicted, among other things, for his responsibility in the enactment of the major anti-Jewish laws of 1938 and 1939, and in preparing the ground for the close cooperation with the Third Reich. During the German occupation, he served as Minister Without Portfolio in Charge of Economic Coordination. Convicted on November 23, 1945, Imrédy was executed on February 28, 1946.[14]

Of greatest interest in connection with the destruction of Hungarian Jewry in 1944 was the trial of the three top officials of the Sztójay government in charge of handling the so-called Jewish question, Minister of the Interior Andor Jaross, and his two State Secretaries, László Baky and László Endre. The "deportation trio," as they were commonly referred to, went on trial on December 18, 1945. By the time it ended on January 4, 1946, Hungary and the world at large had heard the gruesome details on the planning and implementation of the Final Solution. In addition to responsibility for the destruction of the Jews, the three war criminals were also accused of plotting and cooperating with the SS to the detriment of Hungary's national interests. They were sentenced to death on January 2, 1946: Baky and Endre were hanged on March 29, and Jaross was shot by a firing squad on April 14.[15]

Another major trial that aroused great interest was that of Ferenc Szálasi, the leader of the Nazi-type Arrow Cross Party (*Nyilaskeresztes Párt*) and head of the government that was established with German assistance following the anti-Horthy coup of October 15, 1944. He and several leading figures of his regime were charged with crimes against the Jews, especially those of Budapest, and with political and military-related activities that virtually ruined Hungary during their six-months' rule.[16] A major point of the indictment was their collusion with the SS in preventing the Regent from extricating Hungary from the war. The trial also provided details about the evolution of the various Right-radical Arrow Cross (*Nyilas*) movements and parties and about the reign of terror that characterized the Szálasi era.

The last major Hungarian trial of interest in connection with the Holocaust was that of Döme Sztójay, the former Hungarian Minister in Berlin, who had been appointed Prime Minister after the German occupation. It was during his tenure that the Jews of Hungary, excepting those of Budapest, were liquidated. Sztójay's chief codefendants in the trial that began on March 14, 1946, were members of his government, including Antal Kunder, Jenö Rátz, Lajos Reményi-Schneller, and Lajos Szász. Accused of sacrificing the interests of the nation by collaborating with the Third Reich, the accused were found guilty on March 22. Kunder was condemned to life imprisonment; the others were condemned to death and executed shortly thereafter.[17]

Concurrently with these mass trials, the people's courts held individual trials of several persons who had played important roles in the destruction of Hungarian Jewry. Among these were Lieutenant-Colonel László Ferenczy, the gendarmerie officer in charge of the ghettoization and deportation program, and Péter Hain and László Koltay, the leaders of the State Security Police. All three were found guilty and executed in early spring 1946. Their trials were succeeded by those of a relatively large number of officials who had played a "secondary" role in Hungary's political life during the Nazi era.[18]

As in several other countries during the immediate postwar period, the Hungarian authorities also considered indicting the top leaders of the Budapest Jewish Council and of the Zionist-dominated Relief and Rescue Committee "for collaboration with the enemy." Working at top speed on the preparation of war crimes trial cases, the Political and Police Division of the Hungarian State Police of Budapest in fact collected a number of depositions and other evidence toward this end in 1945-46.[19]

A similar plan was under way in Transylvania, where there was considerable bitterness, especially in Cluj (Kolozsvár), against the local wartime Jewish leaders. However, only one member of the Budapest Jewish Council was actually tried. Identified by several of his Council colleagues as an informer in the service of the Hungarian Nazis, Rabbi Béla Berend of Szigetvár was convicted by a people's tribunal in Budapest and condemned to ten years' imprisonment in 1946. A year later, however, NOT reversed the lower court decision and Rabbi Berend was allowed to leave Hungary for the United States.[20] The three lawyer members of the Budapest Jewish Council—Ernö Boda, Ernö Petö, and Károly Wilhelm—were summoned to account for their activities on the Council by the Budapest Bar or Chamber of Lawyers (*Ügyvédi Kamara*), but were eventually exonerated.[21] The controversial role played by the traditional and Zionist leaders of Hungary during the war in general and the German occupation in particular was revealed during the 1953-55 Grünwald-Kasztner trial in Israel (see below).

The Hungarian people's tribunals continued their activities for several years, handling progressively fewer and less important cases. By March 1, 1948, criminal proceedings had been initiated against 39,514 persons, and 31,472 cases had been disposed of. Of these, 5,954 were dismissed and 9,245 ended with not guilty verdicts. Of the 16,273 convictions, 8,041 resulted in imprisonment of less than one year and 6,110 in terms between one and five years. Only 41 individuals were condemned to life terms at forced labor. In the country as a whole, 322 individuals were condemned to death; however, only 146 of these sentences were carried out, while the rest were commuted to life imprisonment.[22] There is no way to determine how many of the convicted criminals were released or had their sentences commuted under the various amnesty programs of the communist regime. György Berend, the former Deputy President of NOT, summed up the record of the Hungarian people's tribunals as follows:

> If one takes into account how many leaders in respectable positions, how many warmongers and agitators against the people, and how many thousands of forced labor company murderer guards and *Nyilas* mass murderers were produced during the 25 years before the liberation, the above statistics elicit serious doubts even in the most ardent opponents of the people's tribunals.[23]

In addition to Hungary, Hungarian nationals accused of involvement in the destruction of Jews—and of crimes against Romanians and Serbs—were also tried in Romania and Yugoslavia. Their trials took place soon after the war and involved crimes committed in

Hungarian occupied Northern Transylvania and the Bácska, respectively.

Romania

In connection with the tragedy of Hungarian Jewry, two trials were held in 1946 in Cluj (Kolozsvár), the capital of Transylvania, in people's tribunals set up under the provisions of Decree-Law No. 312 of the Ministry of Justice, dated April 21, 1945. The structure and organization of these tribunals were basically the same as those of Hungary. In the first of the mass trials, 63 individuals were accused of crimes against Romanians and some Jews during the occupation of Northern Transylvania by Hungarian troops in September 1940.[24] The destruction of the Jews of Northern Transylvania was the subject of the second mass trial, involving 185 individuals. Among these were the government, military, police, and gendarmerie officers and officials of the counties and of the cities that had been involved in the implementation of the Final Solution in the province. The sentences handed down by the court were stiff—20 were condemned to death and many more to life imprisonment. Many of the accused, however, were tried *in absentia*. They represented the group that received the harshest penalties. Among them was Colonel Tibor Paksy-Kiss, the gendarmerie officer in charge of the ghettoization in the province. Of these only a few were eventually tried, mostly in Hungary. None of those condemned to death was executed.[25] Moreover, many of the criminals in custody were freed shortly after Romania's transformation into a Soviet-style people's democracy early in 1948. These were deemed "socially rehabilitated and politically re-educated"; among them were a number of fascists who had been condemned to life imprisonment for crimes against Jews.[26]

Yugoslavia

In accordance with the provisions of Article 14 of the Armistice Agreement, the Hungarian authorities extradited to Yugoslavia several top-ranking Hungarian officers charged with complicity in the massacre of thousands of Serbs and Jews in the Bácska (Bačka), the area occupied by Hungary during 1941-44.[27] The accused, including

General Ferenc Szombathelyi, the former Chief of the General Staff; General Ferenc Feketehalmy-Czeydner, the Commander of the Fifth Army Corps; Major-General József Grassy; and Captain Márton Zöldi, were first tried in Hungary.[28] The trial of the latter two, who were also accused of active involvement in the Final Solution in 1944, began on January 8, 1946. They were condemned to death by hanging four days later. The Hungarian trial of Generals Feketehalmy-Czeydner and Szombathelyi began on March 21 and March 28, respectively. They too were found guilty by the court. All four were then handed over to the Yugoslavs, who retried them together with several Hungarian county and city officials active in the Bácska area during the occupation era. The trial began on October 24, 1946 in Újvidék (Novi Sad), the site of the greatest massacre. All of them were condemned to death six days later. They were executed early in November.[29]

* * *

The destruction of Hungarian Jewry was also the subject of several major war crimes trials that were held in the Federal Republic of Germany (West Germany), Austria, Czechoslovakia, Poland, and Israel. These involved top-ranking Nazi officials associated with the German Foreign Office and the Reich Security Main Office (*Reichssicherheitshauptptamt*—RSHA), especially the Eichmann-*Sonderkommando*.

West Germany

Trials by Non-German Courts. Prior to the emergence of the Federal Republic of Germany as a sovereign entity, the crimes committed against the Jews of Hungary were the subject of the International Military Tribunal at Nuremberg, the 12 cases tried before the U.S. Military Tribunals, and the trials conducted by the British in their zone of occupation. At Nuremberg, the tragedy that befell Hungarian Jewry was dealt with primarily in the cases involving RSHA chief Ernst Kaltenbrunner and Foreign Minister Joachim von Ribbentrop. The Americans brought up the case of Hungarian Jewry in connection with the cases involving Oswald Pohl, the Flick, I.G. Farben, and Krupp combines, and the so-called Ministries cases. The British dealt with it primarily in the case involving Josef Kramer and 44 other defendants associated with the Auschwitz, Natzweiler, and Bergen-Belsen camps. The two other occupation powers, France and the USSR, also held a few war crimes-related military trials that dealt peripherally with the wartime plight of Hungarian Jewry.[30]

By far the most important trial relating to Hungarian Jewry was that of Edmund Veesenmayer, the former Plenipotentiary of the Third Reich in occupied Hungary. As a leading defendant in the Ministries Case (1948), Veesenmayer was convicted on several counts of the indictment and condemned in April 1949 to 20 years' imprisonment.[31] In pursuit of U.S. postwar policy objectives in Germany, John J. McCloy, the U.S. High Commissioner for Germany, commuted Veesenmayer's sentence in January 1951 to 10 years. He was freed a year later on the recommendation of a special U.S. clemency board.[32]

German Trials. The reconstituted German courts held a number of trials that dealt specifically with the tragedy of Hungarian Jewry. By far the most important of these was that of *SS-Obersturmbannführer* Herman Alois Krumey and *SS-Hauptsturmführer* Otto Hunsche, two leading figures of the Eichmann-*Sonderkommando* in Hungary. Though they played a crucial role in Hungary,[33] they lived in Germany undisturbed for 15 years after the war. They were tried and convicted shortly after their arrest in 1960, only to be freed by an appellate court. They were retried in 1964-65 in Frankfurt-am-Main: Hunsche was acquitted, Krumey was sentenced to five years at hard labor (February 3, 1965). On the prosecutor's appeal, the Appellate Court at Karlsruhe nullified the Frankfurt court's decision in 1968 and ordered a new trial. This time Krumey was condemned to life imprisonment and Hunsche was sentenced to 12 years (August 29, 1969). Their conviction was upheld on January 17, 1973.[34]

In the Auschwitz Trial (December 1964 – August 1965), the catastrophe of Hungarian Jewry was discussed especially in connection with the case against Victor Capesius, the Transylvanian pharmacist who had served as Josef Mengele's assistant on the selection ramp in Auschwitz. He was condemned to nine years imprisonment but was freed shortly afterward, following the Karlsruhe higher court's order that the years Capesius spent in internment after the war be counted as part of his sentence.[35]

The West German authorities launched criminal proceedings against three other high-ranking officials of the Third Reich who had played an important role in the destruction of Hungarian Jewry: Horst Wagner and Eberhard von Thadden, the two leading officials of the *Inland II* Section of the German Foreign Office, and Albert Theodor Ganzenmüller, the State Secretary in charge of the railways in the Reich Ministry of Transport. None of them served any time in prison. Thadden was killed in a car accident (November 8, 1964); Wagner, whose trial actually began on May 29, 1972, but was suspended and periodically postponed because of illness, died in Hamburg on March 13, 1977.[36] Ganzenmüller, who was indicted among other things for providing the railroad cars used in the deportation of the Jews, went on trial on May 3, 1973. The trial was first delayed because of his lawyer's involvement in another prolonged case, then indefinitely postponed on medical grounds. Like many other of his Nazi colleagues, Ganzenmüller also escaped punishment.[37] Among the several top-ranking Nazi officials who had served in Hungary during the occupation but were never brought to trial were *SS-Obergruppenführer* Otto Winkelmann and *SS-Standartenführer* Kurt Becher.[38]

Austria

Two of the major war crimes trials held in Vienna related directly to the Holocaust in Hungary. The first one was that of *SS-Hauptsturmführer* Siegfried Seidl, the former commander of the Theresienstadt concentration camp and a leading member of the Eichmann-*Sonderkommando*. In Hungary, Seidl had served as an expert advisor in the roundup and deportation of several large Jewish communities, including those of Eger, Marosvásárhely, Mátészalka, Nyíregyháza, and Székesfehérvár. Found guilty as charged, Seidl was executed in Vienna on October 4, 1946.

The second trial involved *SS-Hauptsturmführer* Franz Novak, the *Sonderkommando*'s transportation expert and liaison with the Reich Ministry of Transport. After living unmolested for 15 years, he was the subject of several trials. In his first trial (November 1964), Novak was condemned to eight years. On appeal, the Appellate Court (*Ober-*

landesgericht) of Vienna nullified the judgment and ordered a new trial. After the second trial, held in September 1966, the court ordered Novak's release a month later because the jury was deadlocked over the issue of "superior orders." After the Appellate Court nullified the acquittal in February 1968, Novak was placed on trial once again on December 20, 1969. Convicted on one count, he was sentenced to nine years' imprisonment. This time, though, the Appellate Court concurred with the appeal by the defense and ordered still another trial, scheduled for August 1971. This fourth trial was held in March 1972 and the jury adopted the position of its predecessor in the first trial. Novak was condemned to seven years in prison on April 13, 1972.[39]

Also of interest in connection with the destruction of Hungarian Jewry was the trial in Vienna early in 1972 of Walter Dejaco and Fritz Karl Ertl, the SS officers and architects who designed and built the Auschwitz gas chambers and cremation furnaces. Both defendants were acquitted and released from custody on March 10, the jury having concluded that they had acted under military orders and were ignorant of the use to which the death ovens would be put![40]

Other Countries

Trials of interest to Hungarian Jewry were also held in Poland, Czechoslovakia, and Israel. In Poland, the liquidation of Hungarian Jewry was a subject in the trial of Rudolf Franz Ferdinand Höss, the former Commandant of Auschwitz. He was condemned to death by a Warsaw tribunal on March 29, 1947, and executed in Auschwitz a few days later.

In Czechoslovakia, the Bratislava trial of *SS-Hauptsturmführer* Dieter Wisliceny, a leading member of the Eichmann-*Sonderkommando* in Hungary, was of special interest. Wisliceny played a determining role in the roundup and ghettoization of the Jews, an expertise he had acquired in the liquidation of the Jewish communities of Slovakia and Greece. Convicted on February 27, 1948, Wisliceny was hanged in Bratislava on May 4.[41]

In Israel, many details of the Holocaust in Hungary—and the tragic fate of European Jewry as a whole—came to light during the trial of Adolf Eichmann, the former head of Section IV.B.4. of the

RSHA. Captured by Israeli agents in Argentina in May 1960, Eichmann was tried in Jerusalem in 1961. He was hanged in Ramla on May 31, 1962.[42]

The catastrophe of Hungarian Jewry was also at the core of one of the most controversial trials ever held in Israel. It involved Rezsö (Rudolph) Kasztner, the former *de facto* head of the Budapest Relief and Rescue Committee—the *Vaadah*. The trial, which started out as a libel suit brought by Kasztner against Malkiel Grünwald, a *Mizrahi* Zionist who had accused him of collaboration, began on January 1, 1954. Intertwined with domestic political and governmental issues, the trial ended with the conviction of Kasztner. In a 300-page opinion dated June 22, 1955, Judge Benjamin Halevi of the Jerusalem District Court concluded that "Kasztner sold his soul to the devil." The judgment of the lower court was reversed by a 3:2 decision of the Supreme Court on January 15-17, 1958, clearing Kasztner of the stigma of "collaboration." However, by that time Kasztner was dead: on March 4, 1947, he had been shot by zealots in Tel Aviv.[43]

The United States and Canada

A few Hungarian nationals were also the subject of judicial proceedings in the United States and Canada. These North American democracies became more sensitive to issues relating to the Holocaust only after the easing of the Cold War in the era of détente. They became increasingly responsive to allegations that they were harboring thousands of individuals who had been actively involved in the Final Solution. Many among these suspected war criminals lived undisturbed for decades, hiding behind the cloak of anonymity. Others, enjoying the support of sundry ultra-conservative elements, prospered openly as frontline champions of anti-communism.

The United States was the first to act, largely as a result of the legislative initiative of Congresswoman Elizabeth Holtzman (D-NY). In 1979, it brought about the establishment of the Office of Special Investigations (OSI) within the framework of the Department of Justice. Relying exclusively on civil proceedings (the United States lacks jurisdiction to bring criminal prosecutions against individuals whose crimes were committed outside the country against non-American citizens), the OSI achieved considerable progress in identifying and taking legal action against Nazi perpetrators residing in the United States. By April 1996, it succeeded in stripping 53 such persons of U.S. citizenship and removing 45 from the United States.

Among these were two former Hungarian nationals: József Szendi, a former gendarme who was involved in the deportation of so-called "alien" Jews in 1941 and participated in the Hungarian anti-Jewish campaign in 1944, and Ferenc Koréh, the former "responsible editor" of *A Székely Nép* (The Székely People), an anti-Semitic daily published in Sepsiszentgyörgy in Northern Transylvania. Koréh was also associated with other anti-Jewish and anti-Allied periodicals and served in the Hungarian Propaganda Office during the Holocaust. After coming to the United States in 1958, Szendi lived and worked as a janitor in Cookeville, Tennessee, until his retirement in the 1970s. It was Szendi's personal vanity that led to his unmasking: he had revealed part of his background in a book published in Hungary shortly after the collapse of the communist system.[44] The OSI initiated denaturalization proceedings against him on September 9, 1992, and on June 18, 1993, the U.S. District Court in Cookville revoked his citizenship. Under an agreement that was not totally unfavorable to him, Szendi "voluntarily" left the United States a few days later and went back to Hungary.

Ferenc Koréh, 86 years of age in 1996, had come to the United States in the early 1950s and worked for several decades after his arrival as a Hungarian specialist for Radio Free Europe. The OSI began denaturalization proceedings against him in the early 1980s, but for some internal reason the case was left dormant until the early 1990s. After lengthy legal wranglings, a Federal District Court in Newark, NJ awarded summary judgment to the U.S. Government in June 1994 after finding, among other things, that Koréh's admitted service as Responsible Editor of the *Székely Nép* constituted "advocacy and assistance in persecution" and "membership and participation in a movement hostile to the United States." The court's order revoking Koréh's citizenship was upheld by the Third Circuit Court of Appeals in Philadelphia on July 14, 1995. On April 19, 1996, the U.S. Justice Department initiated deportation proceedings against Koréh, who at the time of this writing tries to remain with his family in Englewood, New Jersey on grounds of advanced age and illness.

The pitfalls of the criminal approach followed by Canada almost 40 years after the war were revealed in the ill-fated "Finta case" (October 1989 - May 1990). The trial involved Imre Finta, a Hungarian gendarmerie captain who was charged, among other things, with the confinement, imprisonment, and robbery of 8,617 Jews who had been concentrated in the brickyard ghetto of Szeged, one of the largest provincial cities of Hungary, in 1944. As the head of a special gendarmerie investigative unit, Finta was in charge of gendarmes who, often working in plain clothes, interrogated and tortured Jews for the "recovery" of their hidden wealth. He and his gendarmes were also actively involved in the June 25-28, 1944, deportation of the Jews from Szeged.[45]

The trial of Finta was initiated by the Canadian Department of Justice following the recommendations of a special commission headed by Justice Jules Deschenes. According to the commission's report, which was submitted to the Canadian Parliament on March 12, 1987, only 20 of the 882 investigated cases included *prima facie* evidence of war crimes warranting urgent legal action. Shortly after the Criminal Code was amended to make possible the prosecution of these cases, the Attorney General of Canada gave his consent to the indictment of Finta on August 18, 1988, presumably considering his case as the prosecution's strongest. But this trial, in the Supreme Court of Ontario in Toronto, turned out to be an unfortunate test case in the criminal pursuit of suspected war criminals. Although the Canadian Department of Justice made a tremendous effort and invested relatively large sums of money in the collection of documentary evidence, the roundup of witnesses, and the recruitment of a variety of experts, the prosecution could not, more than 40 years after the commission of the crime, satisfy the judiciary requirements of a Western-type criminal court. The jury reached a verdict of not guilty only one day after it was charged on May 24, 1990—an outcome that was upheld by the Court of Appeal for Ontario (April 29, 1992), and the Supreme Court of Canada (March 24, 1994).[46]

A Critical Assessment

The civil and criminal trials conducted in the United States and Canada once again brought to the fore the many still controversial issues concerning the wartime and postwar positions of the Allies on the Nazi-era plight of the Jews. Although fully aware of the details of the Nazis' Final Solution and of the anti-Jewish measures that preceded it, the Allies consistently rejected any active involvement in rescuing of Jews as incompatible with their war aims and strategies.[47] They asserted, not without justification, that their objective—the speediest possible defeat of the Third Reich—was the best possible hope for the Jews as well. Driven by political and strategic considerations, the Allies even refused for a long time to acknowledge publicly, and condemn, the Nazis' pernicious campaign against the Jews. It was not until December 17, 1942, that the Allies issued a declaration acknowledging that the Nazis were engaged in a genocidal campaign against the Jews. Condemning "the bestial policy of cold-blooded extermination," the Allies prudently balanced their inaction on rescue by a declaration of warning against the perpetrators: "[The Allies] reaffirm their solemn resolution to insure that those responsible for these crimes shall not escape retribution, and to press on with the necessary practical measures to this end."[48] The effectiveness of the warning was undercut by its implication that nothing would be done before final victory and by its failure to provide for some immediate threat of retaliation against the Nazis and their accomplices.

The Allies' lamentable record of wartime rescue was largely matched by their postwar record of retributive justice. With the division of the world into two spheres of influence and the emerging Cold War, the Allies effectively reneged on their wartime commitments as they began to reshape their national priorities in accord with their swiftly changing national interests. The Western Allies, eager to develop the areas under their control along democratic, anti-communist lines, became increasingly reluctant to proceed with the prosecution of those actively involved in the Final Solution, including Germans, Austrians, and East European fascist refugees under their jurisdiction. In the new anti-communist climate, they also became progressively more lenient toward those already convicted. As a result of amnesties and arbitrary actions on the part of the occupation authorities, and later of the governments of the reestablished sovereign states, many convicted Nazis had their sentences reduced or were actually freed without going to prison. Moreover, many Nazis and their sundry collaborators involved in anti-Jewish crimes managed to escape prosecution altogether and lived out their lives in various parts of the free world.

The record of the Soviet Union is almost as bleak as that of the Western Allies. Eager to reconstruct their devastated country and develop their own version of communism in East Central Europe, the Soviets also refused to prosecute an unknown number of Nazis deemed useful to their interests. They were particularly lenient toward Nazis with expertise in the sciences, technology, and police security. Moreover, in their eagerness to bring about the transformation of the conquered states into full-fledged people's democracies, the Soviets encouraged the respective communist parties to strengthen their ranks by admitting rank-and-file fascists and Nazi collaborators. Retribution for wartime crimes against Jews was subordinated to the needs of postwar political realities in both spheres of influence.

The belated attempt at retributive justice in the Western world[49] coincided with the drive for the "re-evaluation" of cases involving war crimes and crimes against humanity in the former Soviet bloc nations. Within a short time after the dissolution of the communist system in 1989, the people's tribunals became the subject of heated political debates. More frequent as well as more pointed questions were raised about their legitimacy and the "political" nature of their judgments. Many individuals, especially nationalists on the Right side of the new political spectrum, have argued that the people's courts, lacking constitutional legitimacy, were, in fact, only political instruments of vengeance in the hands of Jews seeking revenge for their alleged wartime suffering. In most of these newly democratic states, well-organized xenophobic nationalist groups have been increasingly active since 1989 in seeking the rehabilitation of their particular wartime pro-Nazi leaders.

The re-evaluation process and the debate over the legitimacy of the people's tribunals seem to have surfaced with particular vehemence in Hungary, as compared to the other former Soviet bloc nations. This is due primarily to the relatively large number of survivors, especially among labor servicemen and the Jews of Budapest, and the disproportionate role some of them played in the immediate postwar security forces. The critique of the people's tribunals' work has become intertwined with an anti-Semitic interpretation of the work in the courts of some of the liberated Jews. Even moderate Christians had distinctly negative views of the disproportionate and highly visible involvement of Jews in Hungary's court and security systems, since no Jews had been permitted to play any role in them during the pre-1945 era. As early as 1948, István Bibó, one of the most respected scholars and statesmen of postwar Hungary, was convinced that one of the primary reasons for the resurfacing of anti-Semitism in post-Holocaust Hungary was the Jews' disproportionate representation in the political police and their identification with the Soviet-imposed communist system.[50] In his view, the presence of a relatively large number of Jews in the people's courts and the security forces gave the impression that Jews were now passing judgment on Hungarians in retaliation for the judgment they had been subjected to in the past. The ends of justice, Bibó argued, would have perhaps been better served if the Jews had voluntarily abstained from being involved in the court and security systems. He was, however, quick to recognize that imposing such an abstention would itself again involve a fascist-type distinction, based on religion, between groups of Hungarian nationals.

There is no doubt that, under the impact of the murder of close to 600,000 Jews, a number of survivors, especially among the former labor servicemen, entered the security forces for vengeance. It is also certain, however, that many other survivors joined these forces, the people's courts, and the leftist movements, in pursuit of justice and the creation of a new, genuinely social-democratic Hungary. The argument over their presence in these organs of state power is tainted by anti-Semitism. Rightist extremists, chauvinistic nationalists, and those who distort or actually deny the Holocaust have endeavored, especially after the collapse of the communist system in 1989, to identify the evils of the Soviet era with the power the Jews allegedly wielded in the instruments of state power.[51] As Shlomo Avineri, a highly respected Israeli political scientist, observed, the reason why Jews became rather visible in the political police forces of the emerging communist regimes was simple:

> After 1945 the main task of the political police in those countries was to trace fascist collaborators and bring them to trial, and to prevent the resurgence of fascist and near-fascist movements. Who but Jews could be trusted not to have been involved in such movements and not to have brothers and cousins and uncles and nephews who were involved? And who but Jewish people had an unquestioned motivation to bring Nazi collaborators and fascists and antisemites to trial? That this would become a pact of the Stalinist devil became clear to many of these people only much later.[52]

And indeed much of the criticism of the people's courts is a reflection of the legitimate critique of the abuses of the Stalinist era. Clearly, the postwar Hungarian trials did not uphold the guiding principles of judicial procedures in criminal cases in well-established democratic societies. But given the governmental vacuum of the immediate postwar era and the fascist character of the Hungarian judiciary system during the Sztójay and Szálasi periods, there was no viable alternative to the establishment of a temporary court system based on the provisions of the Armistice Agreement. As to the accusation that the people's courts lacked constitutional legitimacy and historical continuity, no rational person could expect that the Hungarian courts, which had been dominated by the Arrow Cross before the Soviet forces took over, could have done justice in cases involving war crimes and crimes against humanity.

In retrospect it is clear that the people's courts pursued not only the punishment of those accused of active collaboration with the Third Reich and involvement in the Final Solution, but also longer-range political objectives. With the political strings increasingly in the hands of Soviet-backed communists, the people's courts were also exploited, among other things, to bring about the gradual liquidation of the counterrevolutionary regime that had ruled Hungary since 1919, re-educate the masses along new political-ideological lines, and prepare the ground for the establishment of an anti-fascist, pro-Soviet people's democratic system. It is fair to assume that not all those who were associated with the security forces and the people's courts during the immediate postwar years were privy to these objectives of the so-called Muscovite leaders of the Hungarian Communist Party and their Soviet mentors.

Shortly after the systemic change of 1989, legal measures were started to redress the judicial-political injustices of the past. On January 11, 1994, the Constitutional Court (*Alkotmánybíróság*) of the new democratic republic of Hungary found most provisions of Law VII/1945 (which incorporated Decree No. 81/1945.M.E.) unconstitutional on the grounds that they provided punishment for acts that were not deemed criminal at the time of their commission. It left standing, however, Paragraph 5 of Article 11 and Paragraph 2 of Article 13, which relate to war crimes identified as punishable under both international law and Hungary's criminal code (Law No. IV of 1978).[53]

The ruling of the court resulted in the nullification of many of the decisions of the people's tribunals. As a consequence, an indeterminate number of fascists who had actively participated in various phases of the Final Solution, including police and gendarmerie officers and officials of the Sztójay and Szálasi governments, had their sentences reversed. Feeling officially vindicated, a number of them even received compensation for their suffering "at the hands of the communists." Some, though aged, were actually emboldened to resume their ultra-Rightist, neo-fascist political activities. Providing ammunition for the small but vocal group of "historical revisionists," they are in the forefront of distorting, denigrating, and denying the Holocaust. The elusiveness of retributive justice has once again been matched by the durability of anti-Semitism.

NOTES

1. At the time of the German occupation, the Jewish population of Hungary was 825,000, including the approximately 100,000 converts or Christians identified as Jews under the Nazi laws. According to the census of 1941, the Jews represented 4.94 percent of the total population. The Jewish losses during the Second World War came close to 600,000. See Randolph L. Braham. *The Politics of Genocide. The Holocaust in Hungary* (New York: Columbia University Press, 1994), pp. 1296-1301. (Cited hereafter as Braham, *Politics*.)

2. See *ibid*., chapter 23. See also Martin Gilbert, *Auschwitz and the Allies* (New York: Holt, Rinehart and Winston, 1982), and Walter Laqueur, *The Terrible Secret* (Boston: Little, Brown, 1980).

3. For details on the destruction of Hungarian Jewry, see Braham, *Politics, passim.*

4. On Hungarian Nazis and ultra-rightists who had escaped to the West, see Refs. no. 2335-41 in *The Hungarian Jewish Catastrophe. A Selected and Annotated*

Bibliography, Randolph L. Braham, comp. and ed. (New York: Columbia University Press, 1984). (Cited hereafter as Braham, *Bibliography*.)

5. On the extradition issue, see Jenö Lévai, "The War Crimes Trials Relating to Hungary" in *Hungarian Jewish Studies*, Vol. 2, Randolph L. Braham, ed. (New York: The World Federation of Hungarian Jews, 1969), pp. 263-65. (Cited hereafter as Lévai.)

6. On these Nazis' activities in Hungary, see Braham, *Politics*, *passim*.

7. On the Hungarian suspected war criminals, see Martin Himler, *Igy néztek ki a magyar nemzet sírásói* (This is What the Gravediggers of the Hungarian Nation Looked Like) (New York: St. Marks Printing, 1958), 196 p.

8. The decree went into effect on February 5, 1945. Amended several times, it was formally enacted into law by the Provisional National Assembly on September 14, 1945, as Law No. VII of 1945. For text see *1945. évi országos törvénytár* (National Code of Laws for 1945) (Budapest: Athenaeum, 1945), pp. 33-52.

9. The presiding judges and their deputies were appointed by the Minister of Justice. The lay judges represented the five anti-Nazi political parties constituting the Hungarian National Independence Front (*Magyar Nemzeti Függetlenségi Front*): the Democratic Bourgeois Party (*Demokratikus Polgári Párt*), the Independent Smallholders' Party (*Független Kisgazdapárt*), the Hungarian Communist Party (*Magyar Kommunista Párt*), the National Peasant Party (*Nemzeti Parasztpárt*), and the Social Democratic Party (*Szociáldemokrata Párt*).

10. The people's courts, including NOT and the prosecution offices, were supplanted on January 1, 1952, by new organs of justice established under Law No. III of 1951 of the new pro-Soviet people's democratic regime. For some details, see Braham, *Politics*, pp. 1317-23. See also Lévai, pp. 255-63.

11. The wartime system of labor service in Hungary was unique in Nazi-dominated Europe. For details, see Braham, *Politics*, pp. 284-380. See also his *The Hungarian Labor Service System. 1939-1945* (Boulder, CO: East European Quarterly, 1977), 159 p.

12. For details, see Braham, *Politics*, pp. 198-209.

13. *A Bárdossy per. A vád, a vallomások és az itélet* (The Bárdossy Trial. The Indictment, the Testimonies, and the Verdict), Ferenc Abrahám and Endre Kussinszky, eds. (Budapest: Hiradó Könyvtár, 1945), 64 p., and *Bárdossy László a népbíróság elött* (László Bárdossy Before the People's Tribunal) (Budapest: Maecenas, 1991), 375 p. (With notes and introduction by Pál Fritz.) See also Elek Karsai, *Itél a nép* (The People Judge) (Budapest: Kossuth, 1977), pp. 17-71.

14. On the trial, see *Az Imrédy per. A vád, a vallomások és az itélet* (The Imrédy Trial. The Indictment, the Testimonies, and the Verdict), Ferenc Abrahám and Endre Kussinszky, eds. (Budapest: Hiradó Könyvtár, 1945), 127 p. See also Karsai, *Itél a nép*, pp. 72-119.

15. For the transcript of the trial with comments and notes, see *Az Endre-Baky-Jaross per* (The Endre-Baky-Jaross Trial), László Karsai and Judit Molnár, eds. (Budapest: Cserépfalvi, 1994), 650 p. See also Karsai, *Itél a nép*, pp. 185-215. For details on their role in the Holocaust of Hungarian Jewry, see Braham, *Politics*, *passim*.

16. The Szálasi trial began on February 5, 1946. Along with leading members of his government, including Károly Beregfy, Sándor Csia, József Gera, Gábor Kemény, Jenö Szöllösi, and Gábor Vajna, Szálasi was convicted and condemned to death on March 1. They were all executed later that month. Two of Szalasi's cabinet members, László Budinszky and Count Fidél Pálffy, were tried in December 1945, and executed early in March 1946. For some details, see *A Szálasi per* (The Szálasi Trial), Elek Karsai

and László Karsai, eds. (Budapest: Reform, 1988), 766 p. For details on the Szálasi era in Hungary, see Braham, *Politics*.

17. For some excerpts from the trial, see Karsai, *Itél a nép*, pp. 140-84. For details on the anti-Jewish measures enacted during the Sztójay era, see Braham, *Politics*.

18. *Ibid.*, pp. 1321-22.

19. See, for example, the July 19, 1946, statement by Mrs. László Szántó, née Gabriella Kertész, incriminating Joel Brand and Rezsö Kasztner. This, and several other similar depositions, may be found in file NB. 2600/1946, relating to the trial of Rabbi Béla Berend, a member of the Budapest Jewish Council. See "RG-52 Randolph Braham Collection" in the archives of the U.S. Holocaust Memorial Museum in Washington, D.C.

20. For details on this controversial case and its aftermath, see Braham, *Politics*, pp. 480-89.

21. *Ibid.*, p. 905.

22. Lévai, p. 277. For sources relating to the war crimes trials held in Hungary, see Refs. no. 2022-2315 in Braham, *Bibliography*.

23. Lévai, p. 278. See also György Berend, *A népbíróskodás* (People's Justice) (Szeged: The Author, 1948).

24. Hungary acquired Northern Transylvania from Romania under the so-called Vienna Award of August 30, 1940, imposed by the Axis Powers. For details, see Braham, *Politics*, pp. 167-76.

25. For the records of these and other war crimes trials held in Cluj and elsewhere in Romania, see RG-25.004M in the archives of the U.S. Holocaust Memorial Museum, Washington, D.C.

26. These criminals were freed under the provisions of Decree No. 72 of March 23, 1950. For text see *Buletinul Oficial* (Official Gazette), March 23, 1950. For the English translation of the judgment and details about the proceedings, see Randolph L. Braham, *Genocide and Retribution. The Holocaust In Hungarian-Ruled Northern Transylvania* (Boston: Kluwer-Nijhoff, 1983), 260 p.

27. Hungary occupied the Bácska (also known as the Délvidék) area in April 1941, following the defeat of Yugoslavia by the Germans See Braham, *Politics*, pp. 181-85. On the massacres, see *ibid.*, pp. 214-22.

28. Feketehalmy-Czeydner, Grassy, and Zöldi were originally tried in Budapest in 1943 during the administration of Prime Minister Miklós Kállay. Inasmuch as Hungary was an ally of the Third Reich, the trial of high-ranking officers for murdering Jews and Serbs was an act of great political courage. The defendants were condemned to imprisonment ranging from 11 to 15 years, but they fled the country and found refuge in Vienna as guests of the Gestapo. They returned to Hungary with the German occupation forces in March 1944 and played an active role in the liquidation of Hungarian Jewry. For details, see *ibid.*, pp. 218-22.

29. *Ibid.*, pp. 1324-25. See also Lévai, pp. 288-89.

30. The French courts were primarily concerned with crimes committed in concentration and forced labor camps. Of the Soviet trials, by far the most important from the Hungarian Jewish point of view was that of Franz Jaeckeln, the Higher SS and Police Leader, *Ostland*, who was commander of the forces that slaughtered over 23,000 Hungarian and Ukrainian Jews near Kamenets-Podolsk in late August 1941. Jaeckeln was executed in 1946. For sources relating to the French and Soviet trials, consult *Guide to*

Jewish History Under Nazi Impact, Jacob Robinson and Philip Friedman, comps. (New York: YIVO Institute for Jewish Research, 1960), pp. 190-209 and 209-10, respectively.

31. For the transcript of the trial, see *Ministries Case* (Court 4, Case 11), transcript pp. 2702-50, 3617-59, 7143-58, 13062-460, and 26156-189. See also *Trials of War Criminals Before the Nuernberg Military Tribunals Under Control Council Law No. 10* (Washington, D.C.: Government Printing Office, 1949-1953), Vol. 14, pp. 825-31, 646-60, 812-17, and 858-59. See also Refs. no. 2005-10 in Braham, *Bibliography*.

32. On the composition of the clemency board, see Raul Hilberg, *The Destruction of the European Jews* (Chicago: Quadrangle, 1961), pp. 684-715.

33. See Braham, *Politics, passim.*

34. On these trials, see Ref. nos. 2000-2 in Braham, *Bibliography*.

35. On Capesius and others involved in the destruction of Hungarian Jews, see Bernd Naumann, *Auschwitz. A Report on the Proceedings Against Robert Karl Ludwig Mulka and Others Before the Court at Frankfurt* (New York: Praeger, 1966).

36. On Wagner's and Thadden's activities in connection with the Holocaust in Hungary, see Braham, *Politics, passim.*

37. For some additional details on the trials held in West Germany, see *ibid.*, pp. 1325-28. See also Lévai, pp. 285-88.

38. On their activities during the German occupation of Hungary, see Braham, *Politics, passim.* Winkelmann died in Bordersholm on September 24, 1977. Becher died in Bremen in early August 1995. See also Refs. no. 1943-45 and 2011-16 in Braham, *Bibliography*.

39. Braham, *Politics*, pp. 1328-29. See also Ref, no. 2003 in Braham, *Bibliography*.

40. *The New York Times*, March 11, 1972.

41. For Wisliceny's statement concerning his and the *Sonderkommando*'s role in Hungary, see Doc. 440 in *The Destruction of Hungarian Jewry. A Documentary Account*, Randolph L. Braham, comp. (New York: World Federation of Hungarian Jews, 1963). See also Ref. no. 2017 in Braham, *Bibliography*.

42. For references to all aspects of Eichmann's activities and to his pursuit, capture, and trial, see *The Eichmann Case. A Source Book* (New York: World Federation of Hungarian Jews, 1969), 186 p. See also Refs. no. 1946-95 in Braham, *Bibliography*.

43. On all aspects of the Kasztner case, see Braham, *Politics*, pp. 1088-1112. See also Refs. no. 1911-35 in Braham, *Bibliography*.

44. Szendi's book, titled *Csendörsors. Hernádnémetitöl Floridáig* (Gendarme Fate. From Hernádnémeti to Florida), was published in 1990 by the Miskolc branch of the Hungarian Democratic Forum Party, post-communist Hungary's dominant party at the time.

45. Finta escaped from Hungary in January 1945. He was first tried *in absentia* in Szeged early in 1948, and sentenced to a minimum of five years of forced labor (Szeged, People's Court, Case No. 221/1947/10). He was eventually captured by the Americans, who kept him in a POW camp for 18 months without learning of his background. He emigrated to Canada in 1951, settled in Toronto, and lived as a restaurateur virtually until his indictment for war crimes.

46. On many ramifications of the case, see Randolph L. Braham, "Canada and the Perpetrators of the Holocaust: The Case of Regina v. Finta," *Holocaust and Genocide Studies*, Vol. 9, No. 3, Winter 1995, pp. 293-317. For the Hungarian-language version, see "Kanada és a Holocaust bünelkövetöi. A Regina kontra Finta büntetöper," *Századok* (Centuries), Budapest, Vol. 129, No. 6, 1995, pp. 1331-54.

47. For details about the Allies' awareness of the Final Solution, see footnote 2.

48. "German Policy of Extermination of the Jewish Race," *The Department of State Bulletin*, Vol. 7, No. 182, December 19, 1942, p. 1009.

49. In addition to the United States and Canada, Australia and Great Britain also began to deal with suspected Nazi war criminals in their midst in the early 1990s. In their test cases, they followed the strategy of criminal judicial procedure that had already been used in Canada's Finta case, and ended up with the same negative result.

50. See his "Zsidókérdés Magyarországon 1948-után" (The Jewish Question in Hungary After 1948), *Válasz* (Response), Budapest, No. 8, October-November 1948, pp. 778-877.

51. This is a standard theme of the several Right-radical parties that emerged after 1989 and their press organs.

52. See his "The Return to History and Its Consequences for the Jewish Communities in Eastern Europe" in *The Danger of Antisemitism in Central and Eastern Europe in the Wake of 1989-1990*, Yehuda Bauer, ed. (Jerusalem: The Hebrew University of Jerusalem, 1991), p. 98.

53. For the text of the decision, including its justification, see "A 2/1994.(I.14)AB határozat" (Decision No. 2/1994.(1.14)AB), *Az Alkotmánybíróság határozatai* (Decisions of the Constitutional Court), Budapest, No. 1, 1994, pp. 9-20.

HOLOCAUST STUDIES SERIES

Randolph L. Braham, Editor
The Institute for Holocaust Studies
The Graduate School and University Center
The City University of New York

Previously published books in the Series:

Perspectives on the Holocaust, 1982
Contemporary Views on the Holocaust, 1983
Genocide and Retribution, 1983
The Hungarian Jewish Catastrophe: A Selected and Annotated Bibliography, 1984
Jewish Leadership During the Nazi Era: Patterns of Behavior in the Free World, 1985
The Holocaust in Hungary — Forty Years Later, 1985
The Origins of the Holocaust: Christian Anti–Semitism, 1985
The Halutz Resistance in Hungary, 1942–1944, 1986
The Tragedy of Hungarian Jewry: Essays, Documents, Depositions, 1986
The Treatment of the Holocaust in Textbooks, 1987
The Psychological Perspectives of the Holocaust and of Its Aftermath, 1988
Reflections of the Holocaust in Art and Literature, 1990
Studies on the Holocaust in Hungary, 1990
Anti–Semitism and the Treatment of the Holocaust in Postcommunist Eastern Europe, 1994
The Tragedy of Romanian Jewry, 1994
The Wartime System of Labor Service in Hungary, 1995
The Holocaust in Hungary: Fifty Years Later, 1997
The Destruction of Romanian and Ukrainian Jews during the Antonescu Era, 1997
The Romanian Nationalists and the Holocaust: The Political Exploitation of Unfounded Rescue Accounts, 1998

The Holocaust Studies Series is published in cooperation with the Institute for Holocaust Studies. These books are outgrowths of lectures, conferences, and research projects sponsored by the Institute. It is the purpose of the Series to subject the events and circumstances of the Holocaust to scrutiny by a variety of academics who bring different scholarly disciplines to the study.

The first three books in the Series were published by
Kluwer–Nijhoff Publishing of Boston